The Rise of the Labour Party 1880-1945

Paul Adelman

LONGMAN

LONGMAN GROUP LIMITED
London

*Associated companies, branches and
representatives throughout the world*

© Longman Group Ltd 1972

First Published 1972
Sixth impression 1980
ISBN 0 582 31427 5
Printed in Hong Kong by
Commonwealth Printing Press Ltd

ACKNOWLEDGEMENTS

We are grateful to the following for permission to reproduce copyright
material:

F. W. Bealey for an extract from the *Bulletin of the Institute of Historical Research* Vol. 29, 1956; Ernest Benn Ltd. for an extract from
The Story of the Dockers Strike by H. L. Smith and Vaughan Nash;
Frank Cass and Co. Ltd. for extracts from the *History of the Fabian
Society* by Edward Peace; The Hamlyn Publishing Group Ltd. for an
extract from *My Life's Battles* by Will Thorne; Hamish Hamilton Ltd.
for an extract from *The Trouble Makers* by A. J. P. Taylor; author's
agents for an extract from *Call Bugle Yesterday* by Hugh Dalton and an
extract from *The Fateful Years* by Hugh Dalton; The Labour Party for
an extract from the *Labour Party Manifesto* 1945 — 'Let us Face the
Future'; St. Martin's Press, Inc. and Macmillan, London and Basingstoke for extracts from *Labour and Politics* 1900-1906 by Frank Bealey
and H. Pelling and The Political Quarterly for an extract from an article
by Sydney Webb from *The Political Quarterly* Vol. 32, 1961.

Contents

Introduction to the Series

The seminar method of teaching is being used increasingly. It is a way of learning in smaller groups through discussion, designed both to get away from and to supplement the basic lecture techniques. To be successful, the members of a seminar must be informed, or else – in the unkind phrase of a cynic – it can be a 'pooling of ignorance'. The chapter in the textbook of English or European history by its nature cannot provide material in this depth, but at the same time the full academic work may be too long and perhaps too advanced.

For this reason we have invited practising teachers to contribute short studies on specialised aspects of British and European history with these special needs in mind. For this series the authors have been asked to provide, in addition to their basic analysis, a full selection of documentary material of all kinds and an up-to-date and comprehensive bibliography. Both these sections are referred to in the text, but it is hoped that they will prove to be valuable teaching and learning aids in themselves.

Note on the System of References:

A bold number in round brackets (**5**) in the text refers the reader to the corresponding entry in the Bibliography section at the end of the book.

A bold number in square brackets, preceded by 'doc.' [**docs 6, 8**] refers the reader to the corresponding items in the section of Documents, which follows the main text.

PATRICK RICHARDSON
General Editor

Foreword

In 1880 not one independent Labour member sat in the House of Commons, though there were three working men present, all of whom owed their seats to Liberal votes and supported the Liberal Party. After the general election of 1945, however, 393 members of the Labour Party sat in the House of Commons, and for the first time in its history the party commanded a clear majority of the seats. The aim of this study is to explain how and why this transformation took place. I have in fact tried to answer two questions: why was the Labour Party formed? why did it eventually emerge as the second party in the state, and subsequently His Majesty's Government? On both questions there has been a considerable amount of new material published since the Second World War, not only by historians like Pelling, Marwick, Hobsbawm and Skidelsky, but also, mainly in an autobiographical form, by many of the major participants in the party's later history. Indeed, the last twenty years have seen a virtual renaissance in the study of 'Labour history', marked by the foundation in 1960 of a special Society and Bulletin for the subject. The present book is an attempt to analyse some of this new evidence and the problems it raises for the ' history of the Labour Party.

For some students of labour history there are, in a sense, no problems involved in the study of the Labour Party. For them, once the working men had been granted the vote by the Reform Acts of 1867 and 1884 and made to see the grim reality of their position within capitalist society by the socialists, they were bound to create their own party; and, given their numerical strength, that party was certain eventually to achieve power in the state. The rise of the Labour Party is, therefore, on this interpretation, 'inevitable', and men and events are judged by their contribution to an ineluctable process. These interpretations of Labour history have been, implicitly at least, seriously undermined by the detailed investigations of recent historians, who have shown how far removed from 'inevitability' and how limited was the role of socialism in the formation of the Labour Party, how unrevolutionary were the masses, and indeed how complex and often fortuitous many of the major developments in the party's history were.

Nevertheless, if the rise of the Labour Party was not 'inevitable', there are certain general factors at work in the later nineteenth century which do have an important bearing on its formation. There are, firstly, the profound social and economic changes of the period, notably, the so-called 'Great Depression' (15). The Great Depression was marked by falling prices and profits; but for the working class as a whole — despite the large pockets of heavy unemployment which characterised this period, and the appalling conditions among the unskilled — falling prices meant rising real wages, which lasted until the turn of the century. Rising living standards, linked with political and educational progress and the growth of civic amenities, meant a general raising of standards for at least the 'labour aristocracy'. But this advance was coupled also with a blurring of the lines between the skilled and the unskilled workers as mechanisation and large-scale production destroyed the old craft skills; while the rise of the 'white-collar' worker, as a result of the expansion of trade, finance and the service industries, led to a growing distinction between the middle and working classes, especially in London. All this meant that, in the later nineteenth century, the working class becomes more homogeneous, more concentrated in certain areas, and more class-conscious. Now there is a definite 'labour interest' which, in an age of rising political democracy, rapid economic change and widening social horizons, sought expression and fulfilment.

And these changes in the character of society fitted in with, and partly caused, changes taking place in the realm of ideas. As a result of the writings of economists and philosophers like Cairnes, Jevons, Henry George and T. H. Green, the intellectual justification for *laissez faire* began to crumble, and there was an increased sympathy among the educated and prosperous with the aspirations of working men (17); an attitude of mind which was reinforced by the work of social investigators, like Charles Booth, who showed what a mass of poverty and degradation still lay at the bottom of late-Victorian society. None of these developments made it inevitable that a Labour Party would develop, especially as the Gladstonian Liberal Party still existed as the guardian of the working man's political conscience. But they did make it likely that some thinking men and women would become socialists — and the history of modern Socialism in this country is intertwined with the history of the Labour Party. The so-called 'Socialist revival' of the 1880s is, therefore, perhaps the best starting point for a study of the rise of the Labour Party.

PART ONE

Origins

1   Socialism and Trade Unionism

THE SOCIALIST REVIVAL OF THE 1880s

Between the decline of Chartism in the 1850s and the early 1880s there was no organised socialist movement in Great Britain. Socialism existed, but it was confined almost entirely to discussions in a few obscure working men's clubs, mainly in London, and these were dominated by socialist refugees from the Continent. The greatest of these, Karl Marx, was to die in 1883, almost unknown after thirty years residence in the capital, with not one of his major works yet translated into English. By the end of the decade, however, at least two important socialist societies existed, the Social Democratic Federation and the Fabian Society, as well as a number of splinter groups; and though their total membership was small, their influence was considerable. Socialism, if still a dirty word to the employing and governing classes, could no longer be ignored as an intellectual creed by the thinking public.

The origins of modern British socialism lie deep in the history of mid-Victorian society (28). But there are a number of particular factors which enable us to pinpoint the socialist revival of the early 'eighties. First, there was the growing disillusionment of many radicals with the record of official liberalism: not only Gladstone's tenderness to the Whigs and his reluctance to embark on a programme of further social and political reform, but his apparent continuation of Disraeli's imperialistic policies in Egypt and South Africa; and, above all, the government's support for coercion in Ireland which seemed the utter negation of all that liberalism stood for (6). Secondly, there was the very different influence of the American, Henry George, and his famous work, *Progress and Poverty*, first published in the United States in 1879 and in England the following year. It is difficult for us today to appreciate the extraordinary impact on his contemporaries, particularly in England, of this forgotten man and his unread masterpiece, whose thesis — that the ills of society are due to the 'unearned increment' obtained by the landlord — seems now largely irrelevant to the problems of his age [doc. 1]. But *Progress and Poverty* is that *rara avis*, an economics textbook which became a world best-seller. In England alone in the 1880s Kegan Paul, the publisher, sold 109,000 copies in a cheap sixpenny edition, thus making it 'the greatest single educational force moulding the British working class' (**42**, p. 54). Henry George followed up this publishing success by carrying out a triumphant personal tour of the British Isles in 1881. He was welcomed by the Rev. Stewart Headlam, the Christian Socialist, as 'a man sent from God', and his forceful personality and ethical appeal had a remarkable effect on his audiences. He made five more similar tours during the next nine years.

How are we to account for this unique success? One point may be suggested: *Progress and Poverty* fitted in closely with the mood of the moment among radical circles in England and Ireland. For not only was the year 1879 a year of intense agricultural depression, but the late 'seventies and early 'eighties witnessed in England bitter attacks on the evils of landlordism by a whole variety of land reformers and land reform associations, summed up in Joseph Chamberlain's notorious phrase of 1883 about 'the class that toil not neither do they spin' (**6**, p. 41). In Ireland, unhappily, these attacks were not confined to the written or spoken word. What Henry George did therefore was to make men, particularly working men, think about the contrasts that existed in a society of 'tramps at one end, millionaires at the other'; and, as J. A. Hobson pointed out in an acute contemporary article, to 'give definiteness to the feeling of discontent by assigning an easily intelligible economic cause' (**40**). George was no socialist; but it was an easy transition from the evils of landlordism, through the gospel of land taxation to socialist ideas. It was in this way that Henry George influenced men and women like Bernard Shaw, H. H. Champion, Keir Hardie, H. M. Hyndman and Beatrice Webb, all in their diverse ways to become important representatives of the socialist movement of the 'eighties.

Most of these persons were members of the middle class, and indeed the socialist revival of the 'eighties was primarily a middle-class phenomenon. Hence *Progress and Poverty* is also part of that wider and deeper ferment of ideas which the young Beatrice Webb saw stirring the hearts and minds of so many of her cultivated and prosperous contemporaries, what she called, characteristically, 'the consciousness of sin'.

> I do not mean [she wrote] the consciousness of personal sin . . . the consciousness of sin was a collective or class consciousness; a growing uneasiness, amounting to conviction, that the industrial organisation, which had yielded rent, interest and profits on a stupendous scale had failed to provide a decent livelihood and tolerable conditions for a majority of the inhabitants of Great Britain (**139**, i, 204-6).

It was indeed a distinctly bourgeois figure, H. M. Hyndman, who founded in 1884 the Social Democratic Federation, 'the first modern socialist organisation of national importance in Britain' (92, p. 231). Hyndman was, however, in many ways a curious and contradictory person to head a socialist party. Educated at Eton and Trinity College, Cambridge, he was always conscious of his status as a gentleman, and normally wore the customary top hat and frock coat of members of that class. He also continued his family's associations with the City and, moreover, was a strong supporter of the Empire and British naval power. His political instincts were therefore basically Tory rather than Liberal; and it was his persistent antipathy to liberalism that later cut him off so clearly from the majority of British labour leaders, and often from his own associates. In 1881 he was converted to Marxism after reading *Das Kapital* in a French translation (the first English translation only appeared in 1887) while on a trip to the United States; and in the same year he published his own Marxist exposition, *England for All*. This was in many ways, as Hyndman's latest biographer suggests, 'a text-book of English "Tory Democracy" rather than of continental Social Democracy' (138 p. 42); moreover, it committed the grave solecism of not mentioning the master by name. This annoyed Marx intensely, and he remained aloof from Hyndman until his death two years later; while Engels, as a result of the 'shabby treatment' meted out to his friend and collaborator, maintained his own personal vendetta with Hyndman until his own death fourteen years later.

The origins of the S.D.F., however, lie not in Hyndman's Marxism, but in his opposition to current liberalism. In June 1881 a number of working men from the London radical clubs, together with Hyndman and a group of prominent left-wing Liberals, held an inaugural meeting in London 'to unite, if possible, all societies willing to adopt a Radical programme with a powerful Democratic party'. As a result the Democratic Federation was born; a radical rather than a socialist body, whose interests lay primarily in Irish policy and land reform. But the increasing virulence of Hyndman's opposition to Gladstone led to the gradual withdrawal of most of the Federation's radical supporters, and in 1883 Hyndman, as President, was able to convert it into a purely socialist body: in 1884 it was rechristened the Social Democratic Federation. By that year in fact the society had recruited a number of remarkable young socialists: H. H. Champion, an ex-army officer and, like Hyndman himself, something of a Tory in outlook; Eleanor Marx, her famous father's beloved youngest daughter; Belfort Bax, journalist and Marxist; Tom Mann and John Burns, skilled working men; and — the biggest catch of all — William Morris, artist, poet and designer and, in addition, wealthy enough to help the society financially [**doc. 2**]. It was Morris who became Treasurer of the Federation, with Champion, who owned and edited the newspaper *Justice*, as Secretary.

The major problem for Hyndman and his companions as leaders of an ostensibly revolutionary socialist party was: what tactics should be pursued in order to bring about the socialist revolution? Should the party preach the Marxist doctrine of the class struggle and, relying on growing working-class discontent, lead the embattled proletariat into an immediate conflict with the state power? Or should it rely on a campaign of remorseless Marxist propaganda until, at some future date, the established order collapsed through its own internal contradictions and the working class spontaneously began the socialist revolution? Though Hyndman has often been condemned for his rigid political views, he never came down firmly on one side of the fence or the other. In practice, his policies were a mixture of prejudice, dogma and expediency, as well as a passionate though muddle-headed devotion to the socialist cause; he was, for example, never really prepared to work directly with the trade union leaders, and they in turn were bitterly opposed to his godless and illiberal creed [**doc. 3**].

On the one hand, therefore, Hyndman did his best throughout the 'eighties to spread the gospel of socialism through his own multifarious writings and public debates with prominent radicals like Charles Bradlaugh. The party also produced its own programme of short-term radical reforms – the despised 'palliatives' – land reform, municipalisation, and the rest; and in 1885 (with the help of funds from a Tory agent, Maltman Barry) even put up parliamentary candidates at the unlikely constituencies of Hampstead and Kennington. They polled fifty-nine votes between them, though John Burns did better at Nottingham. On the other hand, even apart from questions of theory, there was much to tempt the S.D.F. in the economic conditions of the 1880s towards more extreme courses. For 1884 and 1886 in particular were years of severe hardship for many sections of the working class; and the S.D.F. members seized the opportunity to help in strike actions in the provinces and, more dramatically, to assume the leadership of the unemployed demonstrations in London, 1886-87. It was in this way that John Burns first displayed his magnetism as a London labour leader. But the agitation was partly discredited by the 'West End riots' in the winter of 1886, which were followed by the well-publicised trial and subsequent acquittal of the S.D.F. leaders – Burns, Champion and Hyndman. This trial of strength with the authorities culminated in the shambles of 'Bloody Sunday' in November 1887, when Trafalgar Square was cleared forcibly by the police [**doc. 4**]. These tactics brought excellent publicity for the S.D.F., but achieved little else since, with the coming of better times later in the year, the agitation died away. Thus 'Bloody Sunday', though it has its place in the martyrology of the British Labour Movement, proved to be an end rather than a beginning. It did, however, lead to important heart-searchings within the Social Democratic Federation itself.

As early as December 1884 a small but important group of members led by William Morris and Eleanor Marx, incensed by Hyndman's domineering methods and extremist tactics, seceded from the society to form the Socialist League. 'As Hyndman considers the S.D.F. his property', wrote Morris, 'let him take it and make what he can of it, and try if he can really make up a bogy of it to frighten the Government. . . . we will begin again quite cleanhanded to try the more humdrum method of quiet propaganda' (123, pp. 222-3).

The loss of Morris's prestige — and his money — was a severe blow to the Federation; and two years later, owing to the electoral scandal over 'Tory Gold', another tiny group left the party. But the worst was yet to come. For in 1887, H. H. Champion, disillusioned with the use of force as a political weapon, came out strongly in favour of building up a more widely based socialist party which would cooperate with the trade unions and appeal directly to the 'labour interest'. Burns and Mann were prepared to back Champion's views; but, despite Burns's attack on 'cliqueism' and 'despotism' at the 1888 Annual Conference of the S.D.F., Hyndman retained his hold over the majority of members, and it was Champion who left the party, taking *Justice* with him, to be followed shortly afterwards by Burns and Mann.

Impressed particularly by the strength and single-mindedness of the Irish Party in the House of Commons, Champion now aimed at pushing forward labour questions at by-elections and increasing the labour representation in the House. His instruments for this purpose were the Labour Electoral Association (founded by the Trades Union Congress in 1886), and his old paper *Justice*, now converted into the *Labour Elector*. His most famous intervention was in support of Keir Hardie at the mid-Lanark by-election in 1888. This campaign, though unsuccessful, helped to begin the 'labour revolt' against the domination of the Liberal Associations, and thus, as Henry Pelling has argued in a sympathetic appraisal, marks out Champion as an important figure in the rise of the Labour Party (131). Unfortunately, his insights were not appreciated at the time, and he was never able in any case to allay completely the working men's suspicions of his earlier Tory associations. His group broke up, and in 1893 he himself departed for Australia, where he died in obscurity in 1928.

Despite these vicissitudes the S.D.F. survived, and Hyndman carried on as undisputed master. By the end of the 'eighties, though the party's membership was still small, it had built up important centres of power among the skilled workers, particularly in Lancashire, and in London where it dominated the Trades Council; moreover, its revelations about labour conditions were beginning to affect the unskilled workers in the capital. It was indeed these aspects of its work, rather than its support for a socialist revolution, that were in the end to be the S.D.F.'s real contribution to the rise of the Labour Party. As Hobsbawm writes: 'Its greatest achievement was to provide an introduction to the labour movement and a training-school for a succession of the most gifted working-class militants' (**92**, p. 232).

The Fabian Society, the other important socialist organisation founded in 1884, emerged out of the ethical Fellowship of the New Life when a group of more socially committed members agreed 'that an association be formed whose ultimate aim shall be the reconstruction of Society in accordance with the highest moral possibilities'. It was when they concluded that this implied *socialist* reconstruction that the Fabian Society, as it came to be called, became a distinctly socialist body. The leading members of the new society were Frank Podmore, E. R. Pease and Hubert Bland; and it was Podmore who thought up the tantalising motto from which the society got its name: 'For the right moment you must wait, as Fabius did most patiently, when warring against Hannibal, though many censured his delays; but when the time comes you must strike hard, as Fabius did, or your waiting will be in vain, and fruitless' (**46**).

They were soon joined by Bernard Shaw, then a struggling young writer, who had in quick succession passed through Georgeism and Marxism; by Annie Besant; and, in the following year, by Sidney Webb and Sydney Olivier, both young clerks in the Colonial Office, who were recruited by Shaw. There were also other less serious recruits, as the latter recalled: 'It was a silly business. They had one elderly retired workman. . . . There were anarchists led by Mrs Wilson. There were young ladies on the look-out for husbands, who left when they succeeded. There were atheists and Anglo-Catholics' (**48**). In its early days in fact there was no clearcut distinction between the Fabian and other socialist societies (especially in the provinces), and members often could and did belong to more than one group. But the London Fabian Society soon developed a distinctive flavour of its own — middle-class, intellectual, vivacious, tolerant and slightly otherworldly — which was to colour its whole history, and which Shaw has captured so marvellously in his letters and writings of this period [**doc. 5**]. As Shaw says, justifying his own decision to join the Fabians, it was 'an instinctive feeling that the Fabians ... would attract the men of my own bias and intellectual habits ... we were then middle-class all through, rank and file as well as leaders' (**49**, pp. 130-1).

What then, given this common ethos, were the basic ideas of the Fabians? Two main influences helped to shape Fabian thought. First, there was the English liberal-utilitarian tradition, as exemplified particularly by the writings of John Stuart Mill. But to this native tradition there was added a strong tincture of Marxism: not Marx's economic views (which the Fabians rejected in favour of Jevons's marginal utility theories), but his conception of historical change and the nature of capitalist society. It was this historical and sociological insight that made the Fabians true socialists rather than just radicals of the school of Morley or Chamberlain which they could so easily have become; and this, as McBriar argues, enables us to see them as a genuine part of the European socialist movement (**45**).

The starting point of Fabian thought, therefore, was their view of capitalist society. Capitalist society was, they believed, as contemporary evidence showed in overwhelming and appalling detail, an unjust and also an inefficient society. But just as capitalism had itself evolved out of feudal society, so contemporary capitalism, under the impact of technological and institutional change, democracy, and the pressures generated by working-class discontent, was itself evolving, through increasing state intervention and municipal enterprise, into a socialist society. 'There will never be a point', wrote Annie Besant in *Fabian Essays* in 1889, 'at which a society crosses from Individualism to Socialism. The change is ever going forward; and our society is well on the way to Socialism' (**37**, p. 141). For the Fabian, indeed, socialism meant basically state and municipal socialism — 'Gas-and-Water Socialism', in the famous phrase; a view which reached its *reductio ad absurdum* in Sidney Webb's extraordinary account in *Fabian Essays* of the remarkable victories being totted up each day for socialism, as the state enlarged its control over 'dairies, milk-shops, bakeries, baby-farms, gasometers, schools of anatomy, vivisection laboratories, explosive works, Scotch herrings and common lodging-houses' (**37**, pp. 45-6). This view is, however, just as clear in the more concise statement of the Society's programme [**doc. 6**].

Since socialism was, as it were, 'implicit' in contemporary capitalist society — 'an interpretation of the spirit of the times', in Edward Pease's phrase — the Marxist (and S.D.F.) doctrine of the inevitability of revolution was both irrelevant and absurd: rather, the 'inevitability of gradualness' was a fact of life. The task of the Fabian Society, therefore, was to make the transition to socialism as painless and effective as possible through the conversion of society, not with emotional rhetoric and street brawls, but with rational factual socialist argument; and this implied a reliance on peaceful democratic methods which in any case, as Sidney Webb argued, fitted in with the traditions of the British people [doc. 7]. For the Fabians then, unlike the S.D.F., there was no great problem of tactics. The primary aim of the Society was to convince men, and especially men of influence, of the truth of the socialist case. Hence the major role of the Society was as a socialist fact-finding and fact-dispensing body: through lectures, discussion groups, research and writing, hobnobbing with the Establishment, writing reports and speeches for working men, acting as members of and giving evidence before committees and commissions, publishing the *Fabian Essays* of 1889 (which sold 27,000 copies within two years) and, above all, by the endless stream of *Tracts* on every conceivable subject of social concern — *Facts for Londoners, Questions for Poor Law Guardians, Socialism and Sailors, Allotments and How to Get them*, to name but a few — which sold in their thousands. 'The Fabians' aim was, therefore', as Beatrice Webb wrote, 'to make thinking persons socialistic', rather than 'to organise the unthinking persons into Socialist societies' (**140**, p. 32).

The latter point is particularly significant. The Fabians were strongly against the idea of establishing an independent socialist or labour party. Their aims could be realised most easily, they believed, by a policy of winning over the leaders of the established political groups — the famous policy of 'permeation'.

This permeation [wrote Sidney Webb] is apparently destined to continue, and the avowed Socialist party in England will probably remain a comparatively small disintegrating and educational force, never itself exercising political power, but applying ideas and principles of social reconstruction to each of the great political parties in turn (**76**, p. 30).

Much has been made of the success of this policy of 'permeation', particularly by Shaw, who attributes to it the acceptance of the radical 'Newcastle Programme' by the Liberal Party in 1891; the sympathetic policies of the *Star* newspaper; the reforms of the London County Council; and, as he tells us in his best buttonholing manner, the adoption of the programme of the Independent Labour Party at Bradford in 1893 which 'I settled with him (Keir Hardie) in two minutes conversation as we crossed one another on the stairs' (**49**). Most of these claims, however, have been exploded by presentday historians like

A. M. McBriar and Paul Thompson. It is worth pointing out that one Fabian essayist, Hubert Bland, though his views were ignored by his colleagues at the time, poured scorn not only on Webb's conception of socialism, but on the whole policy of permeation. It was a delusion, argued Bland, to imagine that the holders of wealth and power would voluntarily 'go socialist'. 'There is', he wrote, 'a true cleavage being slowly driven through the body politic', and the only solution for socialists was to establish a real party of their own (37, p. 195). This the Fabian Society never really accepted: not in 1893, and not even with any great enthusiasm in 1900.

What then was the contribution of the Fabians to the formation of the Labour Party? Despite the noble efforts of Margaret Cole and Anne Fremantle (35, 38), the 'Little Band of Prophets' has had a rough handling recently from professional historians. 'No major political development can be attributed with certainty to Fabian influence', writes Professor McBriar (45, p. 349); 'the achievements of the Fabian Socialists have been grossly exaggerated' (80, p. 296), writes Paul Thompson; while Professor Hobsbawm, subjecting them to a severe Marxist scrutiny, decides that 'they must be seen not as an essential part of the socialist and labour movement . . . but as an "accidental" one . . . they had . . . no place in the British political tradition' (92). This is rather harsh. For the real contribution of the Fabians lay in those fields for which their unique talents best fitted them: as formidable writers and debaters and superb and often highly successful propagandists for the ideas of 'evolutionary socialism'.

Despite the glittering array of talent displayed by the socialist societies in the 1880s, and the energy and devotion of their members, the total number of socialists in the country by 1889 was still tiny — hardly more than two thousand all told. By contrast, the number of trade unionists in that year was about three-quarters of a million. Yet both the S.D.F. and the Fabians were anti-union: the S.D.F. because of the unions' 'conservatism', the Fabians through arrogance and an obsession with political 'permeation'. It was, however, changes within the trade union movement, that were to inaugurate the next great phase in the history of British labour.

OLD AND NEW UNIONISM

The trade union movement of the 1880s, despite the stresses and strains caused by a rapidly changing social and economic environment, was still shaped basically by the organisation, institutions and ethos created during the heroic struggles of the 'sixties and early 'seventies (102).

Traditionally, membership of a trade union was the prerogative of the skilled worker who had 'served his time'; and it was indeed the great craft unions of engineers, masons, spinners and carpenters, with their elaborate systems of rules and regulations and their high subscriptions and social benefit schemes, which formed the backbone of the movement. In the Trades Union Congress, formed in 1868, and its offspring, the Parliamentary Committee, formed three years later, it possessed a central organisation which could claim to speak for and defend the interests of the whole body of organised workers; and in the 1870s the creation of these new institutions seemed abundantly justified by the passing of the great Trade Union Acts of 1871 to 1876 which appeared to give the trade unions all that they wished for in terms of legal rights and the enforcement of strike action.

Politically too Labour now achieved some recognition. The enfranchisement of the urban workers by the Second Reform Act of 1867 was followed in 1874 by the election of the first two working men members of Parliament; and by 1886 there were nine such members, sitting as 'Lib-Labs', prepared to speak up on labour questions but in all other respects sticking closely to the Liberal Party line (87). Thus the T.U.C.'s policy reflected, in Roberts's words, 'the philosophy of unions whose members were craftsmen, conscious of their skill and standing in the community as worthy, respectable and independent citizens. The unskilled workers were regarded as being of another class' (106, p. 128).

It is true that, as Cole argued in opposition to the Webbs (86, 111), the official trade union leadership of the mid-Victorian period was not as firmly wedded to the principles of *laissez faire* and pacific policies in politics and industrial relations as had formerly been imagined. Nevertheless, it is clear that during the 'eighties at least, the trade union 'old gang' became more complacent, more particularist, and more ostrich-like in their refusal to face up to the profound problems of technological change, demarcation disputes, and unemployment, that now faced the world of labour. 'A kind of deadly stupor covered them', wrote Tom Mann and Ben Tillett, two of their bitterest critics, 'and they really appeared to be dying of inanition' (99, p. 4); while John Burns, their colleague in running the Great Dock Strike, dismissed the craft unions as 'mere middle and upper-class rate-reducing institutions'. Nor did their representatives in Parliament show any greater insight or independence. They were content to be, in Engels's scornful phrase, 'the tail of the Great Liberal Party', though Henry Broadhurst, the leader of the group, gloried in his liberalism and personal devotion to Gladstone.

Secretary of the Parliamentary Committee of the Trades Union Congress between 1875 and 1890; Liberal member of Parliament; and, for one brief glorious moment in 1886, Under-Secretary at the Home Office – the first working man to be appointed to a government post, it was Henry Broadhurst above all who typified, in all its strength and in all its weakness, the attitude of mind of the Trade Union Establishment. Beatrice Webb wrote of him at the T.U.C. Congress in 1889 in her usual vitriolic style: 'A commonplace person: hard-working no doubt, but a middle-class philistine to the backbone: appealing to the practical shrewdness and high-flown, but mediocre, sentiments of the comfortably-off working-man ... he lives in platitudes and commonplaces' (**140**, p. 22).

It was against this type of trade unionism that the so-called 'new' unionism of the period 1889-93 reacted: 'new' because (so the orthodox version runs) it was 'open to all, free from friendly benefits, militant, class-conscious, and socialist'. Moreover, this new unionism began, it is often argued, with the spontaneous explosion of wrath against their wretched conditions that took place among the unskilled workers of the East End of London in 1889, and which led to the Great Dock Strike. This is to pinpoint the movement too precisely. For the London dockers had been active in the early 'seventies, even though the movement soon faded away (**97**); and militancy and organisation were already taking place among seamen and labourers in the north of England, mainly under the aegis of Havelock Wilson, in the early 'eighties. In the same year as the Dock Strike the miners made a great leap forward by forming the Miners' Federation of Great Britain, which covered most unions outside Northumberland, Durham and South Wales. Nevertheless, it is impossible to underestimate the importance of the Great Dock Strike of 1889. It was not only the most dramatic, but also the largest strike in a year relatively free from industrial strife; and one which was significant not only because of its intrinsic interest and symbolic importance as an example of new unionism in action, but because of its wider repercussions both on trade unionism and the labour movement generally (**84**). The prelude to the Dock Strike came, however, in 1887, when the match-girls at Bryant and May's factory in East London, mainly as a result of the activity and propaganda of the socialist Annie Besant, formed a union, came out on strike for better conditions, and won their case (**109**). Two years later, early in 1889, Will Thorne, a stoker at the Beckton Gasworks in East Ham, formed a Gasworkers' Union which gained rapid and widespread support. When they demanded the eight-hour day, astonishingly the owners granted the demand without a struggle [**doc. 8**]. The excitement and enthusiasm aroused among the gasworkers by this success was bound to spill over into dockland, since there were close links between both groups of workers, and between their leaders. Thorne was a member of the S.D.F. and so was Ben Tillett who had begun, not very successfully, to organise a General Labourers' Union among the dockers – 'the despair of the social reformer, and the ghosts of the milk-and-water politician'; and Tillett, together with other socialists like Eleanor Marx, Burns and Mann, had also helped Thorne organise the Gasworkers' Union. The East End of London by midsummer 1889 was therefore a key centre of socialist cooperation and agitation.

In August 1889, as a result of a trivial dispute in one of the London docks, the whole labour force (including the skilled stevedores and watermen who had their own well-organised unions) came out on strike, in support of the famous 'dockers' tanner' (sixpence an hour) and improvements in working conditions. In the first days of the strike Ben Tillett, whose Labourers Union now increased its membership by leaps and bounds, took the leadership on his own shoulders; but when the dock owners refused to negotiate and it became clear that a hard struggle lay ahead, he was soon joined by Tom Mann and John Burns, all three proving themselves outstanding labour leaders [**doc. 9**].

The strike arrangements were conducted in an orderly and peaceful fashion. Relief schemes were organised, and attention was focused on the dockers' grievances by vast processions through the City which won much sympathy and support from the public and the Press. At the same time negotiations were begun between the two sides by the Lord Mayor and, later, Cardinal Manning, who thus became a key figure in the strike. When, in the fifth week, with their resources almost at an end it looked as if the dockers would have to yield, an unexpected grant of £30,000 from Australian trade unionists (compared with £4,500 subscribed by their English brethren!) gave them fresh heart and the wherewithal to carry on. This gave an impetus to new negotiations, and the strike was soon brought to an end in early September with the men gaining, in Burns' famous phrase, 'the full round Orb' of the dockers' tanner, and practically all their other demands.

'The regeneration of the Trade Union Movement', wrote Ben Tillett in his *Memoirs*, 'dates from this great social event' (**136**, p. 117). Certainly the Great Dock Strike gave a considerable stimulus to the growth of new unionism both in London and the provinces in the course of the next two years; though it was not the only factor at work since both economic expansion and (as Hobsbawm has shown) technical changes in particular industries like the gas industry produced their own momentum towards unionisation (**92**). Hence, labourers' and dockers' unions were organised in London and the provincial ports; Havelock Wilson's Seamen's and Firemen's Union shot up to 65,000 members; Thorne's Gasworkers' Union spread to the provinces; the Trades Councils movement blossomed and became an important centre of socialist and new unionist influence; and unskilled workers on the railways and in the building industry, for example, began to be organised. 'The masses are on the move', wrote Engels, 'and there is no holding them any more. The longer the stream is dammed up the more powerfully will it break through when the moment comes' (**18**, p. 523). Yet, under the general euphoria produced by the success of the Dock Strike, the bitter aftermath is often forgotten. 'The Great Dock Strike had attracted world-wide attention; yet twelve months later Tillett's union was eased out of the docks with scarcely a ripple of public interest' (**84**, p. 71). And what was true of the London dockers was true also of provincial dockers' and seamen's unions. By 1893-94 new unionism was in full retreat. Why was this?

One important reason was the onset of depression after 1891; for the unskilled worker in industry was as usual the first to be sacrificed by the employers, and his link with trade unionism, tenuous at the best of times, could hardly survive a prolonged period of unemployment. But another important cause was the beginning of a counterattack organised by the employers, and particularly the dock employers and shipowners, who worked together to resist the unions' demand for the 'closed shop' and further benefits, and to destroy their influence over the dockers and seamen. Poor leadership, and internecine disputes between the different unions, played into the employers' hands; but in addition the latter began to introduce 'free' — that is non-unionist — labour into the docks, often under police protection, which the unions found it difficult to circumvent. Thus between 1890 and 1893 strikes took place at nearly all the major ports, principally to enforce the 'closed shop', and all were defeated. The last and greatest was at Hull in 1893 and, as *The Times* commented: 'At Hull, as elsewhere, the New Unionism has been defeated. But nowhere has the defeat been so decisive, or the surrender so abject' (**84**, p. 81). By the end of the year union membership among the unskilled was rapidly melting away.

Yet new unionism survived. It survived in the 1890s among those unions ·which, like Thorne's union and the transport workers' unions, were organised in expanding industries — gas, water, electricity — often municipally owned and therefore with a built-in interest in stable conditions. These unions too were generally better led than their counterparts in the docks; and indeed, faced with problems of survival and growth, they began gradually to approach nearer to the organisation and outlook of the craft unions. They became more selective in their methods and, like the gasworkers, began to rely 'more on their foothold in certain industries and large works, than on their ability to recruit indiscriminately' (92, p. 187). As a result of this more élitist approach they developed social benefit schemes; and, even more important, began to use their indispensability as 'specialised' labourers to obtain union recognition from the employers, indulge in the tactics of collective bargaining, and thus obtain better working conditions. Hence in the 1890s the frontiers between 'old' and 'new' unionism began to become blurred, at least from an industrial point of view, especially when *all* trade unionists — engineers and miners as well as dockers and seamen — found themselves menaced not only by the new employers' counterattack, but also by a series of disquieting legal judgments. In such a situation the old conceptions of new unionism (both contemporaries' and historians') seem not only inaccurate but irrelevant. For the new unions, with a total membership of something between 100 and 200,000 during this decade, recruited only a tiny fraction even of the vast mass of unskilled labourers, and therefore formed only one small unit in a growing trade union movement which by 1900 numbered about two million members.

But though in the end perhaps the success of new unionism, industrially, was not as great as its supporters had hoped for, politically it was of considerable importance. 'It marked', wrote Ben Tillett, 'the beginning of that close alliance in thought and purpose between the Trade Union Movement and the Socialist Movement which produced in due time the Labour Party' (136, p. 116). For there was a natural affinity between the ethos of new unionism, with its emphasis on working-class solidarity and support for state action, and the ideals of the socialists [doc. 10] ; a union which was symbolised by their common support for the first London May Day in 1890, marked by the singing of the new socialist hymn, the Red Flag [doc. 11] . As we have already seen, socialists like Eleanor Marx, Annie Besant, H. H. Champion, Will Thorne, Tillett, Burns and Mann played a vital part in the first successful phase of new unionism. Naturally enough, many of the new labourers' unions continued to look to socialists for their leaders. But the enormous prestige gained by the socialists from the *annus mirabilis* of 1889 also helped to make the revival of unionism among, for example, the railwaymen, the boot and shoe operatives of the Midlands, and the West Riding woollen workers, more socialist in outlook. Even the great craft unions were not unaffected by the changing mood. In 1891, for example, Tom Mann stood for the Secretaryship of the Amalgamated Society of Engineers and was only narrowly defeated after a hotly-fought contest. In 1892, however, the Union agreed to change its rules and relax the rigid qualifications for membership, a victory described by one labour paper as 'one of the most encouraging signs of the progress of Socialist thought and action in trade unions' (**84**, p. 143). Moreover, the flourishing trades councils, up to 1895 directly affiliated to the T.U.C., were peculiarly associated with the socialists and the new unionists; and in one way or another therefore during this period the socialists were increasing their influence within the trade union movement as a whole. This clash between old and new ideas was bound to be reflected within the Trades Union Congress itself.

Yet the cross currents and struggles within the T.U.C. during the key decade 1889-99, cannot be seen simply as a clash between a reactionary 'old guard' trying desperately to cling to power, and an idealistic group of new unionists supporting socialism and an independent labour party, predetermined to triumph: the intriguing career of John Burns shows the dangers of such a superficial view (**124**). Partly, of course, the clash was just a clash of generations; but, as Dr Duffy has argued, even before 1889 the 'old guard' was not entirely unaffected by the new winds of change blowing in the 'eighties which were already undermining the hardline opposition to the principle of state intervention in industrial matters (**89**). Between 1885 and 1887, for example, the three presidential speeches at the T.U.C.'s Annual Conferences all spoke in favour of the eight-hour day and land nationalisation, and criticised the capitalist system. Yet, with that sublime capacity for contradictory behaviour which is so typical of the T.U.C., Congress up to 1889 threw out by large majorities such typically collectivist resolutions; while the first real direct attack on the 'old gang' — Keir Hardie's blistering personal denunciation of Henry Broadhurst at the 1887 Congress — was easily brushed aside by the old diehard by relying on the deeprooted instincts of working-class loyalty and his own record of service to the movement. As George Howell commented, in words which probably echoed the feelings of most trade union delegates during these years: 'The distinguishing trait in the conduct of prominent "new leaders" has been, and is, their persistent, cowardly, and calumnious attacks upon the old leaders, upon men who have borne the brunt of labour's battles' (**93**, pp. 133-4).

Nevertheless, despite appeals to personal loyalty and the past, the pressures of the socialists could not be denied. They controlled after all about one-quarter of the votes at the T.U.C. in 1890, and it was then that the real clash between the 'old' and 'new' unionists came. Even in physical appearance, suggests Burns, they were different:

Physically the 'old' unionists were much bigger than the new. . . . A great number of them looked like respectable city gentlemen; wore very good coats, large watch chains, and high hats, and in many cases were of such splendid build and proportions that they presented an aldermanic, not to say a magisterial form and dignity. Amongst the new delegates not a single one wore a tall hat. They looked workmen; they were workmen (**102**, p. 104).

It was at the 1890 Congress that, as a result of support from the Miners' Federation and the cotton unions, the tide began to turn in favour of the eight-hour day, the symbol of new unionism; and, partly as a result, Broadhurst resigned as Secretary of the Parliamentary Committee.

Yet, despite the passing of an eight-hour day and other collectivist resolutions between 1891 and 1893, and the election of Burns and Havelock Wilson to the Parliamentary Committee, it soon became clear that the socialists were not to be allowed to have things all their own way. Fenwick, the new Secretary, was a man of the Broadhurst stamp, and he was easily re-elected to the post annually until 1894. He was then replaced by another miner, Sam Woods, who was in favour of the eight-hour day which was now official trade union policy. It was at this point that the majority of members of the Parliamentary Committee (all Lib-Labs) decided to carry through a *coup d'état* and limit socialist influence by changing the system of representation and voting at Congress. It was agreed, therefore, that from 1895 trades councils' delegates should be completely excluded; the 'block' vote principle would be introduced in union representation (one vote per thousand members); and that no one should be a delegate who was not working either at his trade or as a permanent paid official of his union. This last clause had the effect of excluding Hardie and also, ironically, Broadhurst! 'Thus at the time of their greatest strength in Congress which they claimed had been won for socialism, the "new unionists" could not prevent its machinery from being changed to their disadvantage' (**84**, p. 257).

Politically too, despite the setting up of the Labour Electoral Committee in 1886, and the socialists' call for more effective labour representation in Parliament, which was accepted in principle by the 1892 Congress, there was little change in practice in the T.U.C.'s attitude. After the election of 1885 there had been eleven labour men sitting in the House of Commons, all as Liberals. Even after the election of Hardie, Burns and Havelock Wilson to Parliament in 1892, the position remained basically unchanged, since only Hardie out of the dozen labour representatives acted as a truly independent member; Burns and Wilson soon began veering towards the Liberal Party. The labour group remained, therefore, in the taunting words of Jöseph Chamberlain, 'mere fetchers and carriers for the Gladstonian party' [**doc. 12**]. By 1895 it was abundantly clear that the majority of trade union leaders had not yet accepted the need for independent labour representation in Parliament, let alone socialism: yet without their support such policies were impracticable. It was Keir Hardie, above all, among the socialists who saw how imperative it was to obtain the support of the trade unions in the task of establishing a genuinely independent labour group in Parliament. This indeed was to be the primary task of the Independent Labour Party which he had helped to form two years earlier, in 1893.

2 The Formation of the Labour Party

THE INDEPENDENT LABOUR PARTY

By the early 'nineties a recognisably socialist movement had at last been established in Great Britain. In London, the Fabian Society continued its work of 'permeation' and proselytisation among the middle classes, and more than seventy provincial branches were in existence, though these, as Edward Pease, the Society's Secretary, pointed out disdainfully, were strongly working-class in outlook and 'Fabian only in name' (46). The Social Democratic Federation, as we have seen, despite recriminations and secessions among the leadership, continued under Hyndman to build up power and influence in London especially, where it became the dominating socialist force. Its offshoot, the Socialist League, though it had had some influence among the northern miners in 1887, was now a tiny and dwindling body since William Morris had left it in 1890 after it began to be captured by anarchists. All these groups had emerged out of the socialist revival of the 'eighties, and were the creation mainly of middle-class ideas and middle-class aspirations.

What was especially significant, however, in the early years of the new decade was the emergence of an independent labour movement in the north of England, based on factory, mill and mine, and fundamentally working-class in origin, aims and outlook. Its centre was Bradford where, partly as a result of the harsh times suffered by the woollen weavers as a result of the American McKinley tariff of 1890, strikes had occurred over wage cuts, and small labour and socialist clubs had developed which eventually joined together in the spring of 1891 into the Bradford Labour Union. Similar groups were soon formed throughout the West Riding and parts of Lancashire, strongly supported by northern labour newspapers like John Burgess's *Workman's Times*, and Robert Blatchford's *Clarion*, which was started at Manchester in 1891 and, owing to Blatchford's journalistic genius, soon became the most entertaining and popular socialist newspaper in the country (134). It was Blatchford who helped to found the Manchester Independent Labour Party in the following year, though it soon became clear that politics was not his *métier*. The characteristic of all these new groups was their socialism, their working-class character, and, above all, their desire to maintain a rigid political independence from the other two parties. The importance of this new approach seemed to be justified when, in the general election of 1892, Hardie, Burns and Havelock Wilson were returned as labour candidates for West Ham, Battersea and Middlesbrough respectively, and Tillett, though unsuccessful, obtained the respectable total of 2,749 votes at West Bradford. Independent Labour candidates, it now seemed clear, could capture votes from both Conservatives and Liberals, and win elections.

Many socialists now felt, therefore, that the time had come to weld these small socialist and labour groups into a new national party – an Independent Labour Party. Hardie had been thinking on these lines even before he donned his famous cloth cap and entered the House of Commons in 1892. He had hoped to win over Burns – in most respects the obvious choice for leadership of such a party – to his views. But Burns, 'a prey to egotism of the most sordid kind', as Beatrice Webb noted in 1893, was no longer interested: he was already beginning to steer that lonely course that was eventually to take him into the safe harbour of the Local Government Board in the Liberal Government of 1906. It was Hardie, therefore, who now became the major figure in the attempt to form such a party. He had come a long way since his birth in a Kirkshire village in 1856, the illegitimate son of a Scots servant girl and a ship's carpenter. His early years were marked by grinding hardship and poverty from which, like so many future Labour leaders, he only escaped – in body though never in spirit – by taking up trade union activity among his fellow miners and reading widely on 'the social question'. He soon became a socialist and, on a trip to London on union business in 1887, he decided to join the S.D.F. In the end, however, he could not bring himself to do so; and the reasons he gives for his decision – he was obviously repelled by the beery, irreverent, cocksure atmosphere of the London S.D.F. clubs – are important not only for the understanding of Hardie's character and his characteristically ethical conception of socialism, but as an illumination of the profound differences that were soon to develop between London and provincial socialism generally (133).

In the same year, as we have seen, Hardie, as 'the harbinger of the new unionism', made his famous onslaught on Broadhurst; and in the following year, ostentatiously rejected by the local Liberal Association, he stood as Labour candidate at the Mid-Lanarkshire by-election. He failed to be elected; but his disgust with the attitudes of official liberalism, and his growing concentration on labour questions, led him to form in the same year, 1888, the Scottish Labour Party. 'It was', as K. O. Morgan suggests, 'the Scottish labour movement that was to provide the framework for his social and political outlook' (**127**, p. 8). By the time he became a member of Parliament in 1892 he had thought deeply about the nature of the new Labour Party that he believed must come in England. Its members must, he insisted, be completely independent of the other parliamentary parties, a point of view that was well illustrated by his own dogged behaviour in the House of Commons up to 1895. The party must, further, put labour questions first and foremost and aim therefore at obtaining the support and cooperation of the trade unions. 'I am anxious and determined', said Hardie, 'that the wants and wishes of the working classes shall be made known and attended to in Parliament' (**133**, p. 26). But it must, on the other hand, be a party which was not necessarily limited to a working-class membership or dominated by a narrow sectional attitude.

The first move in the formation of such a party was made by Joseph Burgess in the spring of 1892 when, through the columns of his *Workman's Times*, he appealed for the formation of Independent Labour groups in towns and cities throughout the land. The response was immediate and enthusiastic, particularly in the great working-class centres of the north, though a few groups were also formed in London and the south. The problem now was to join them together in a national organisation, and in the autumn a committee was established under Hardie's leadership which arranged for a conference of interested groups to be held at Bradford early in the new year. The choice of Bradford is easily understood. With its twenty-three labour clubs, it was the citadel of provincial socialism; but it also symbolised the roots of the new party: 'The I.L.P. began as it continued, determinedly provincial' (**88**). This was seen in the character of the 120 delegates who assembled at the Bradford Labour Institute on 13 January 1893. The labour clubs, the Fabians, the S.D.F., the Scottish Labour Party, and a few trade unions, all were represented; but the overwhelming majority of the delegates came from the north of England, and more than a third were from Yorkshire. The importance of provincial socialist opinion was further emphasised by the absence of Mann, Burns (who refused to attend), and Champion, who was prevented by illness; while, though the Fabians agreed to send delegates, their attitude, as exemplified by Shaw, their chief representative, was one of total scepticism about the value of the whole venture, though in the end Shaw did perform valuable work in the deliberations of the Conference.

When it came to the practical arrangements for the establishment of the new party, the Conference decided, deliberately, to exclude the word 'socialist' from the title, which was to be called simply, the Independent Labour Party, in order not to discourage trade union support. Nevertheless, the party *was* to be distinctly socialist: its object, 'to secure the collective ownership of the means of production, distribution and exchange' was passed by an almost unanimous vote. The emphasis in the programme that followed was, again quite deliberately, on *economic* measures: abolition of child labour, provision for the sick and disabled, work for the unemployed etc., though political and other points were added later. The Conference decisions on party organisation were less happy. A weak unwieldy Central Executive of fifteen was established, including Shaw, Aveling, Burgess, Mann, Champion and Hardie, with Shaw Maxwell as the elected Secretary. The Executive did control the Central Election Fund; but, owing to the establishment of provisional divisional Councils, it soon became clear that it would be difficult to prevent the local branches going their own way. These arrangements concluded the work of the Conference which ended, we are told, with Keir Hardie beginning the singing of Auld Lang Syne, 'and then the delegates, all joining hands, sang the two verses with considerable precision and much heartiness, following it with three cheers for the Independent Labour Party' (**75**, p. 122).

Despite the enormous enthusiasm that attended the formation of the Independent Labour Party, its first few years were difficult and disappointing. There was lack of money, and the difficult task of supervising and unifying innumerable local bodies was rather beyond the powers of the Central Executive, even after it was reorganised and Tom Mann became Secretary of the party in 1894. These problems, together with the problems of policy-formation, were worsened by the inevitable clashes among the intensely individualistic and wayward men who composed the leadership (**63**). Then both the Fabians and the S.D.F. refused to affiliate; indeed, Beatrice Webb denounced the I.L.P. as 'a wrecking party', checkmating the more reasonable policy of permeation (**140**, p. 117). But since practically all the provincial Fabian Societies *did* join the new party, the London Fabians' animosity could be regarded as mere sour grapes; for, as Ramsay MacDonald told Edward Pease, 'London Socialism . . . is almost as sickly now compared with provincial robustness as London life itself is' (**76**, p. 49). This was certainly not true of the S.D.F., which was a real rival to the I.L.P. in London where the latter, for a variety of reasons, always remained weak. There were also the tricky problems of electoral 'independence', and the hostility of the Liberal Party which was often exacerbated as a result. This was seen in their opposition to the choice of a working-class Liberal candidate in the Attercliffe by-election of 1894, a decision which finally drove Ramsay MacDonald to break with the party and join the I.L.P. All these factors made it difficult for the Independent

23

Labour Party to become a mass party; and it looked, unhappily, as if it would degenerate into merely another small socialist society.

Nevertheless, in the north of England, and particularly in the West Riding of Yorkshire, the gospel of socialism and labour independence was spread by a devoted band of serious-minded hard-working members, including the young Philip Snowden, later the first Labour Chancellor of the Exchequer [doc. 13]. Their outlook stamped its imprint on the I.L.P. which, in Snowden's words, 'derived its inspiration far more from the Sermon on the Mount than from the teachings of the economists' (132, i, 63). Nor were their efforts unrewarded. On town councils and local school boards, and in by-elections, the I.L.P. made headway; while the publication of Blatchford's *Merrie England* in 1894, which sold three-quarters of a million copies, and his encouragement of the Clarion Movement (a cross between the Salvation Army and the Youth Hostels Association) proved that working men were prepared to listen to a cheerful, colourful, down-to-earth socialism [doc. 14]. Despite much local optimism, however, the election of 1895 was a disaster for the I.L.P. All twenty-eight candidates — including Hardie, who neglected his own constituency at West Ham to concentrate on the national campaign — were defeated. Hardie refused to be downcast. 'Despondency? No, no, rather proud, savage elation. Half the battle won the first time, and that, too, the most difficult half. But we must learn how to fight elections' (75, p. 168). The next two years were years of political apathy among the working class, and bickering, disunity and growing despondency within the socialist ranks. Beatrice Webb wrote that:

To us public affairs seem gloomy; the middle-classes are materialistic, and the working-class stupid ... whilst the Government of the country is firmly in the hands of little cliques of landlords and great capitalists and their hangers-on. The social enthusiasm that inspired the intellectual proletariat of ten years ago has died down and given place to a wave of scepticism about the desirability, or possibility, of any substantial change in society as we know it' (140, p. 195).

'By 1897', as Pelling says, 'it was clear that the Socialist boom was over' (75, p. 179). Yet during the next three years we see growing sympathy within the trade union movement for the idea of independent labour representation; and in 1900, as the direct result of a resolution passed by the Trades Union Congress, the Labour Representation Committee was established for just that purpose. How are we to explain this *volte face*?

THE CONVERSION OF THE UNIONS

One major reason was the acceleration of the employers' counterattack against trade unionism in the later 1890s, directed now, not against struggling new unions, but against the aristocrats of the trade union world — coal, cotton, engineering. This was due not only to the difficulties encountered by many employers in an increasingly competitive world market, which led to the inevitable demand for wage cuts; but also to their belief that attempts to increase British industrial efficiency by the introduction of new machinery and new methods, particularly in the engineering industry, were being deliberately held up by the restrictive practices of the A.S.E. and other craft unions. Hence British employers looked longingly across the Atlantic to the United States where they ordered these things better. As Colonel Dyer, President of the Engineering Employers' Federation, put it: 'The federated engineering employers are determined to obtain the freedom to manage their own affairs which has proved to be so beneficial to the American manufacturers. . . . This is what they are contending for' (4, p. 156). From his point of view, the skilled unionist, worried in any case by heavy unemployment in some industries in the 1890s, felt impelled to resist the attempt to reduce him to the status of a machine-minder, and introduce redundancy into the bargain. In addition, trade union leaders (and important sections of public opinion) were appalled by the prospect of American-type trusts proliferating over here, and the brutality and corruption in industrial relations that often accompanied them (47, ch. 5). It was, however, the employers who seized the initiative in preparing for the coming industrial struggle.

They had a number of weapons at their disposal. One of the most significant developments of the period was the growth of employers' associations, both local and national, in most important trades, on the lines of the Shipping Federation of 1890 which had worked so successfully in combating unionism in the docks in the early 'nineties. Probably the most important of these associations was the Federation of Engineering Employers, founded in 1894; and this was followed, four years later, by the foundation of the Employers' Federation's Parliamentary Committee, which brought together representatives of most of the major British industries to act for them in exactly the same ways as the T.U.C.'s Parliamentary Committee acted for the trade unions. Another weapon developed by the employers was the use of 'free labour'. 'Free labour' had been successfully used in the dockside disputes of 1890-93, but its organisation was now made more formal and more efficient by the setting up in 1893 of the National Free Labour Association under William Collison, to protect 'the general body of

Labour from the tyranny and dictation of socialistic Trade Union Leaders'. Collison, a shrewd engaging cockney, who was himself an ex-busdriver and trade unionist, was probably quite sincere in his anti-unionist views (117), though his organisation, it seems fairly certain, was financed by a number of employers' associations. Collison and his associates used every opportunity to attack trade unions, through public meetings, publications, the Press, and the courts of law; but the main function of the Free Labour Association was to provide blackleg labour when needed in industrial disputes. Yet, though the N.F.L.A. had some success in the later 'nineties against weak unions, its overall impact was not very great since skilled labour, in engineering disputes for example, could not easily be replaced; and, as John Saville says, 'it is the political context within which it operated that underlines its significance' (107).

The year 1893 saw two major lockouts as a result of attempts by coal and cotton employers to impose wage cuts in their industries; disputes which were only ended by government intervention and conciliation in the case of coal, and the imposition of the important wage-fixing 'Brooklands Agreement' in the case of the cotton industry. Two years later the employers won a similar conflict with the boot and shoe operatives in the Midlands. But the most important industrial struggle of the decade was the great engineering lockout of 1897-98, since here the toughest of employers' federations faced the greatest of craft unions, and one which, as shown by its rule changes and the election of the I.L.P. man, George Barnes, as Secretary in 1896, was becoming increasingly militant. The dispute began with the engineers' attempt to extend the eight-hour day; but it soon became linked with the whole question of technical change and managerial control within the industry, and was thus followed by a lockout imposed by the employers between July 1897 and January 1898. The struggle assumed a symbolic importance. Both sides in industry — organised labour and organised capital — saw the two protagonists as fighting for *their* interests as a whole. 'A stand must be made for the common good against the common enemy', said George Livesey, a prominent gas company director and notorious anti-unionist, 'This stand is now being made by the engineering employers' (41, p. 158). 'If the workmen are defeated', wrote the journal of the Boot and Shoe Operatives, 'it will have far-reaching results to all other trades' (75, pp. 195-6). In the end, the employers won over the immediate issues in the dispute; but the A.S.E., like all the other craft unions who were the victims of the employers' counterattack, survived to fight another day.

The employers soon received an important ally in their struggle to limit the power of the unions. In 1899 the Appeal Court decided in the important case of Lyons *v.* Wilkins to limit drastically the right of picketing by a trade union, thus seriously undermining the unions' conception of 'peaceful picketing' as secured, they had always assumed, by the legislation of 1875-76. This decision, as Pelling has suggested, was due primarily, not to judicial bias, but to technical changes in the interpretation of the law (**26**, ch. 4). Nevertheless, when coupled with a number of similar decisions in the course of the next year or two, and the bearing these were bound to have on the employers' deliberate use of 'free' labour during this period, it seemed evident to many trade unionists that the very foundations of their movement were once again (as in 1867) under attack. What could they do? Industrial action had failed, and they were helpless against the law. The only solution seemed to be an appeal to political action, something which the I.L.P. had been compaigning for since 1893.

From the Conservatives of course nothing could be expected. Their position was unassailable after the great electoral victory of 1895; and their attitude was, naturally enough, strongly pro-employer. But the benefits of the 'auld alliance' with the Liberals, even for many traditional-minded union leaders, seemed less attractive now than they had done in the heyday of Gladstone. In 1895 the Liberal Party had suffered a disastrous electoral blow, and was now reduced to a weak squabbling parliamentary party, dependent on the votes of the 'Celtic fringe' and supporting policies — Disestablishment on the one hand, Liberal Imperialism on the other — which made no appeal to the industrial working classes (**6**). Moreover, leading nonconformist employers, many of whom held key positions in the provincial party organisations, were often conspicuous for their anti-trade union attitudes; and the growing suspicion of labour leaders for the Liberal caucus was further reinforced by the refusal of many local Liberal Associations to countenance working men as parliamentary candidates, as at Attercliffe in 1894, and elsewhere. Threlfall, Secretary of the Labour Electoral Association, denounced the average Liberal Association as 'a middle class machine ... hampered with class prejudice' (**84**, p. 280). Nor indeed was the labour movement getting much parliamentary representation in return for the mass trade union vote they placed at the disposal of the Liberal Party. 'The verdict on this record cannot be favourable ... in a period in which their membership rose from three-quarters of a million to just over two millions, they had only been able to increase their parliamentary representation from eight to eleven' (**84**, p. 285).

There was much to be said, therefore, for the unionists using their votes independently of the other two political parties; and the development of party politics in local government during the later nineteenth century shows how successful this policy could be. Between 1882 and 1892 labour members on local bodies increased from twelve to 200; and by 1895 there were 600 Labour members on borough councils, many of them socialists. West Ham in 1898 was the first local authority to go Labour, as a result primarily of local socialist (mainly S.D.F.) organisation (80). Nor was the problem of labour representation in Parliament primarily one of money. It is true that members of Parliament were still unpaid – the Liberal Government of 1892-95 had blandly ignored the growing demand for payment of members – but the trade union movement in 1900 controlled funds of over £3 million, and Hardie was elected for Merthyr Tydfil in 1900 with an expenditure of only £300. These were the sort of facts that impressed the socialists in the last five years of the century; and, despite the numerical decline of both the I.L.P. and the Fabians during these years (the S.D.F. on the other hand was booming) and the change in the T.U.C.'s rules in 1895, the socialists were still increasing their influence in individual unions and, through them, on the T.U.C. itself. As a result therefore of socialist 'permeation' of the unions, coupled with the logic of events – the employers' counterattack, judicial decisions, Liberal weakness and hostility – even the oldfashioned trade unionist could no longer oppose the arguments in favour of more independent labour representation with complete conviction. What converted him was not socialism, or indeed any conception of a wider social purpose; but, quite simply, fears for the security of traditional trade unionism.

By 1896 Keir Hardie had already been thinking of a national conference of socialists and trade unionists to push for independent labour representation, and by 1899 the T.U.C. was beginning to think more favourably of the suggestion. This was partly the result of the disastrous defeat of the engineers in the previous year which led the T.U.C. to establish a General Federation of Trade Unions, to coordinate their strike funds, thus laying down an important precedent for united political action. Hardie therefore considered the time was now ripe to push ahead; and the I.L.P. Council appealed to the Parliamentary Committees of both the English and the Scottish T.U.C.s 'with a view to securing united political action'. The Scots responded with a special conference held at Edinburgh which strongly endorsed Hardie's ideas. In England the initiative was seized by the Railway Servants who passed the famous resolution which was to be put before the 1899 Trades Union Congress:

That this Congress, having regard to its decisions in former years, and with a view to securing a better representation of the interests of labour in the House of Commons, hereby instructs the Parliamentary Committee to invite the cooperation of all the co-operative, social-istic, trade union, and other working organisations to jointly cooperate on lines mutually agreed upon, in convening a special congress of representatives from such of the above-named organis-ations as may be willing to take part to devise ways and means for securing the return of an increased number of labour members to the next parliament (**75**, pp. 204-5).

At the Congress this resolution was introduced by James Holmes of the Railway Servants, and seconded by James Sexton of the Liverpool Dockers; and after a vigorous three hours debate it was passed by a vote of 546,000 to 434,000. Seven major unions, mainly under socialist influence, voted for: the Boot and Shoe Operatives, Carpenters, Rail-way Servants, the two Dockers Unions, the Gasworkers and the National Amalgamated Union of Labourers. Their votes totalled only 229,597; while the votes of the big coal and cotton unions who voted against totalled 351,140. It seems likely, therefore, that, even despite abstentions, most of the smaller unions voted for the motion. Yet, even more significant than this in contributing to the success of the motion, as the recent historians of trade unionism argue, was the fact that on this occasion the Lib-Labs were neither united nor prepared to use all their power to destroy the case for increased labour representation (**84**, p. 303). Whatever the causes of the victory, it was a decision which, in Pelling's words, 'revealed a real change in the attitude of the unions to political action' (**75**, p. 206).

Following the passing of the resolution, a small committee repre-senting the trade unions and the socialist societies met together and arranged for the summoning of a conference to discuss the problems of organising increased labour representation. This met in London on 27 February 1900, at the Memorial Hall in Farringdon Street, and it is this meeting that has been looked upon as marking 'the foundation of the Labour Party'. One hundred and twenty-nine delegates were present, representing the socialist societies and a small number of 'advanced' trade unions — less than half those affiliated to the T.U.C. The I.L.P. delegates, as at Bradford, prevented the S.D.F.'s attempt to bind the Conference to socialism and the class war; and they then passed Hardie's motion, the most important of the Conference, to establish:

a distinct Labour group in Parliament, who shall have their own whips, and agree upon their policy, which must embrace a readiness to cooperate with any party which for the time being may be engaged in promoting legislation in the direct interests of labour, and be equally ready to associate themselves with any party in opposing measures having an opposite tendency (75, p. 209).

In this ambivalent fashion the principle of an independent parliamentary party was established, but the details of programme and policy were left to be filled in later. The Conference then established the Labour Representation Committee, consisting of two I.L.P. members, two S.D.F., one Fabian and seven trade unionists, to run independent labour candidates, financed, however, by the separate societies which were affiliated to the Committee. Ramsay MacDonald, who had proved himself an able administrator and was eager for the post, was appointed unpaid Secretary.

All this represented an enormous triumph for the I.L.P., and apparently for the socialists generally, since the trade unions, in a gesture of abnegation, allowed them to be represented on the Committee out of all proportion to their numbers. Little notice was taken of these events, the country being in the middle of the Boer War; and the Fabian Society as usual was pessimistic about the outcome. Nevertheless, as the *Clarion* said: 'At last there is a United Labour Party, or perhaps it would be safer to say, a little cloud, no bigger than a man's hand, which may grow into a United Labour Party' (75, pp. 210-11).

THE LABOUR REPRESENTATION COMMITTEE

Progress in the first year of the Labour Representation Committee was bitterly disappointing. 'They had formed', writes Professor Poirier, 'only a federation composed of organisations, not a party to which individuals might directly adhere' (76, p. 87); and, unhappily, partly due to the glacial pace at which the wheels of trade union machinery turned, union affiliations were slow to take place. After one year, less than a dozen trade unions had affiliated, representing only about 350,000 members (out of a total union membership of two million), and including not even all those who had attended the Memorial Hall Conference. This was a particularly grave hardship since the L.R.C. depended for its income on the subscriptions of affiliated organisations which, at the rate of ten shillings per 1,000 members, was low in any case; and this meant that it could neither afford to have paid officials nor to contribute much directly to election expenses. The consequences were seen in the 1900 general election which followed soon after the Committee's foundation. Fifteen candidates were put forward, sponsored and almost entirely financed by the affiliated trade unions and the socialist societies. Only two were elected: Keir Hardie, and Richard Bell, General Secretary of the Railway Servants, though the latter was, apart from his special interest in railway questions, really a Liberal. In addition there were eight Lib-Labs, four less than in 1895. Under these circumstances it was ludicrous for the L.R.C., with its minuscule membership, to claim to speak for 'Labour'; nor was Hardie able to turn the handful of working-class members into a truly independent labour group in Parliament. Outside the House of Commons, Ramsay MacDonald, as Secretary of the Labour Representation Committee, worked hard and skilfully at the difficult task of wooing the trade unions, maintaining the formal independence of the L.R.C. and, with one eye on the future, keeping lines open to the Liberal Party. He saw, however, that what was essential if the L.R.C. was not to die of anaemia was a large blood transfusion of members and money from the trade unions. This the Taff Vale decision was now to provide.

In June 1900 a group of employees of the Taff Vale Railway Company in South Wales, hoping to seize the opportunities presented by the South African War to improve their conditions and obtain union recognition, handed in their notices and came out on strike. Their action was unofficial, though they had been egged on by James Holmes, a local militant official of the Amalgamated Society of Railway Servants; but, contrary to the advice of Bell, the strike was recognised officially by the A.S.R.S. The company replied by bringing in blackleg labour, and issued summonses against the strikers who had come out in defiance of their contracts; an injunction was also issued against the railwaymen's union itself to restrain unlawful picketing. Settlement of the strike was fairly quickly reached, and by the end of August the men agreed to return to work under the old conditions. But the legal action against the Railway Servants continued; and in September 1900 Mr Justice Farwell upheld the company's injunction against the union, on the grounds that they were liable for the actions of their agents. Though this was reversed by the Court of Appeal in November, it was finally upheld by the House of Lords in July 1901:

Has the legislature [asked Lord Macnaughten] authorised the creation of numerous bodies of men, capable of owning great wealth and of acting by agents, with absolutely no responsibility for the wrong they may do to other persons by the use of that wealth and the employment of those agents? In my opinion Parliament has done nothing of the kind. I can find nothing in the Acts of 1871 and 1875 ... to warrant such a notion (84, p. 315).

The Lords' decision made it possible for the Taff Vale Company to proceed with an action for damages against the Railway Servants, and in December 1902 it was awarded £23,000 plus costs. Thus, for virtually a whole year, from the summer of 1900 to the summer of 1901, the eyes of the trade union world were on the Taff Vale Case. Trade unions, it now appeared, were liable for damages in a corporate capacity. But the full implications of this judgment (and the reaffirmation of the decision limiting picketing in Lyons *v.* Wilkins) were only seen in a series of smaller cases in the course of the next eighteen months, and the realisation by the trade unions, with mounting horror, that in the end the total cost of the Taff Vale case to the Railway Servants would be £42,000. 'Defeated at the polls and attacked in the courts, it appeared that the trade union movement had no alternative but to turn to direct parliamentary action' (**54**, p. 83).

Hardie and MacDonald quickly saw the opportunities that this presented for the Labour Representation Committee. When, as a result of Hardie's parliamentary questioning in August 1901, it became clear that Salisbury's Government intended to do nothing legislatively to help the trade unions, Ramsay MacDonald wrote to them on behalf of the L.R.C. stressing that: 'The recent decisions of the House of Lords . . . should convince the unions that a labour party in Parliament is an immediate necessity' (**54**, p. 77). This view did receive considerable support at the T.U.C. Conference a month later, since for nearly a year the official trade union leadership had shown itself incapable of coming up with an agreed and easy solution of the problems posed by the Taff Vale decision; while, as the parliamentary debates on the subject in the following year showed, their Liberal allies were either unenthusiastic for, or pessimistic about the outcome of, a new trade union Bill. And all this took place against a background of increasing pressure from the employers, and persistent attacks by the Press (particularly *The Times*) on the restrictive activities of the unions.

Politically, it looked as if the trade unions would have to go it alone. The effect of the Taff Vale Case was seen, therefore, in the considerable and rapid increase in trade union affiliations to the Labour Representation Committee. This occurred in two main waves. Between 1900 and the summer of 1901, forty-one unions affiliated, bringing the total number of members up to 353,070; between the spring of 1902 and the winter of 1903, as a direct result of the Lords' judgment (linked also with the ending of the Boer War and a renewed interest in domestic affairs), 127 new unions joined, including the Engineers and the Textile Workers, thus raising the membership to 847,315. The allegiance of the Textile Workers was particularly important, since it meant not only an accession of 103,000 new members to the L.R.C. (the biggest single gain to date) but also showed the effect of Taff Vale even on moderate unionism. Later in 1903 the rest of the building workers came in, and — a portent of the future — the first of the miners' unions, the Lancashire and Cheshire Miners' Federation. ♦

The year 1903 marks, therefore, the real turning-point in the history of the Labour Representation Committee. For the L.R.C. had not only vastly increased its membership and, as a concomitant, its income also, but had gained considerably in prestige and self-confidence. It was therefore able to consolidate its position at its Third Annual Conference in 1903 by increasing the subscription for affiliated societies, which meant that by the end of the year its annual income was approaching £5,000, and establishing a compulsory parliamentary fund for the payment of M.P.s. This also provided an effective way of making members of Parliament and parliamentary candidates toe the party line, especially after the reaffirmation of the principle of 'independence' vis-à-vis the other parties. It was over this issue that Richard Bell was finally expelled from the party in 1905.

All this meant that, despite its small parliamentary membership, the L.R.C. was now a powerful party in its own right, able to draw on the allegiance of an increasing body of voters in the country at large. Of this the Liberal Party leaders, with their eyes on the by-election results and the next general election, were acutely aware; just as, from their point of view, MacDonald and Hardie were impressed by the gains that might be made by 'arrangements' with the Liberals in particular constituencies. Hence the relationship between the L.R.C. and the Liberal Party was to become of vital importance during the three years that led up to the general election of 1906.

Something of a *rapprochement* was already taking place between the two parties during the later stages of the Boer War, as it became clear that, over the nature and conduct of the conflict, the I.L.P. and the anti-imperialist section of the Liberal Party saw eye to eye. Ramsay MacDonald had already begun to think of local agreements with antiwar Liberals, when the whole problem of the Liberal/L.R.C. relationship was seen in microcosm at the North-East Lanark by-election in 1901. There, Robert Smillie, the President of the Scottish Miners' Federation, stood as a Labour candidate (supported by all the antiwar forces) in opposition to official Liberal and Conservative candidates; as a result, the vote was split in a former Liberal seat and the Conservative got in. Herbert Gladstone, the Liberal Chief Whip, read the signs. 'We *must* try to hit it off with the Labour people', he wrote to Campbell-Bannerman, the party leader, 'who are not really unreasonable ... Lanark may be a pretty warning' (**54**, p. 130).

33

Gladstone realised, as he pointed out, that the real difficulty in the way of such agreement was the attitude of the local Liberal Associations, many of whom were still persisting in their opposition to working men candidates. But a series of important by-election results drove home the lessons of North-East Lanark, and made the Chief Whip increasingly aware of the even greater problems that could arise from cold-shouldering the L.R.C.

In August 1902 David Shackleton, Secretary of the Cotton Workers, was returned unopposed for the weaving constituency of Clitheroe as L.R.C. candidate; in March 1903 Will Crooks won a straight fight against a Conservative candidate at Woolwich, thus strengthening MacDonald's hands in his negotiations with Herbert Gladstone; and in July, Arthur Henderson of the Ironfounders won a seat from the Liberals in a three-cornered contest at Barnard Castle. Moreover, both Shackleton and Henderson were recent ex-Liberals. Campbell-Bannerman therefore expressed his approval of seeking an electoral agreement with the L.R.C. Ramsay MacDonald, from his side, began negotiations with Gladstone through the latter's secretary, Jesse Herbert, on the general understanding that Labour would support a future Liberal government, while the Liberals in return would refrain at the next general election from fighting certain selected seats where L.R.C. candidates would stand [doc. 15]. On this basis a detailed agreement was concluded between MacDonald and Gladstone in August 1903; in secret, since both men felt the need to keep the details from their own 'irreconcilables'. By this electoral pact the L.R.C. was given a free hand in some thirty constituencies, and in return MacDonald agreed to support Liberals in other constituencies and a Liberal Government if elected. For both sides the agreement had considerable attractions. For the Liberals it meant the easing of their financial burden (since the L.R.C. controlled an Election Fund of £150,000) and the possibility of winning many urban seats; for the L.R.C. it guaranteed the return of a considerable group of Labour members. For both Gladstone and MacDonald, however, it was a practical bargain: neither could visualise the deeper consequences that ultimately followed.

The electoral arrangement between the L.R.C. and the Liberal Party was the counterpart on a wider scale (and in secret) of what was happening within the House of Commons itself. Keir Hardie still hoped to convert the Labour members in the House (whose numbers had increased to fifteen by 1905) into an independent group; but their growing antipathy to the policies of the Conservative Government and the inhibitions imposed on MacDonald and Hardie by the existence of the secret agreement with Gladstone produced a natural gravitation towards the Liberals. On education, on 'Chinese slavery', on imperialism, the attitude of the Labour group was virtually indistinguishable from that of the Liberal Party; and when, after the resignation of Joseph Chamberlain in September 1903, the defence of Free Trade was added to this list, the understanding between the two parties became closer. In any case, the resignation of Chamberlain seemed to presage the impending break-up of the Conservative Party; and therefore, with the scent of electoral victory already in their nostrils, it was a case for the official Liberal and Labour leadership of 'no enemies on the Left'. To all these topics was added the issue of trade union legislation. For in 1903 the Trades Union Congress, boycotting Balfour's proposed Royal Commission on the subject, came down firmly at last on the extremist side and supported a parliamentary Bill for granting trade unions complete immunity from actions for damages as a result of strike action; and the parliamentary Labour group worked hard to convert the Liberal Party to this policy.

All these political developments, and particularly the emergence of a clearcut labour solution to the Taff Vale problem, led to something of a honeymoon period between the Lib-Labs and the L.R.C. members in the Commons, who drew closer together. In 1905, for example, it was agreed that each group would support the other's candidates at the next general election; and indeed in the last months of the dying Parliament the Labour members sat as one group in the Commons under the chairmanship of John Burns. On the other hand, the increasing friendliness between the L.R.C., the trade unions and the Liberal Party during these years, led to inevitable grumblings from the rank-and-file members of the Independent Labour Party, especially as the I.L.P., after a period of decline, was now rapidly increasing its membership in the country. The cry of 'Socialism betrayed' had already led to the disaffiliation of the S.D.F. in September 1901, and the Fabians' attitude to the L.R.C. was, in Pease's phrase, one of 'benevolent passivity'. Hence the I.L.P. socialists felt, not without cause, that they were in danger of being swallowed up by the trade union Leviathan. The plain fact of the matter was that in terms of men and money the socialists *were* only a tiny minority within the L.R.C.; but, even after 1906, I.L.P. discontent was to bubble away until they finally withdrew from the Labour Party in 1932. These deeprooted problems, however, could easily be ignored in 1905, for in November of that year Balfour finally resigned. Campbell-Bannerman then formed a Liberal Ministry, and all the parties prepared for the coming general election to be held in January 1906.

That election, despite the almost religious aura with which it was surrounded by a later generation of Liberals, had nothing millennarian about it. Its issues were neither original nor inspiring. They were those which had emerged during the last five years of Conservative rule: Imperialism, Tariff Reform, the new Education Act. The L.R.C. programme, apart from a somewhat greater emphasis on social reform, followed the Liberal Party in making the condemnation of these policies the keynote of its election campaign [doc. 16]. The L.R.C. put up about fifty candidates, and, owing to the electoral pact of 1903, it was given a clear run in thirty constituencies, though few concessions were made by the Liberals in South Wales, Yorkshire or the north-east, and none in Scotland. In the end, twenty-nine L.R.C. candidates were successful, mainly in Lancashire where, owing to the protectionist issue, there was a strong swing against the Conservatives. Indeed, the L.R.C. probably gained considerably from its identification with the Liberal cause; and, as Burns said of its candidates, 'many of them were elected by Radical enthusiasm, Liberal votes and trade union funds'. Balfour suggested in a famous remark that Campbell-Bannerman was 'a mere cork dancing on a current which he cannot control' (**54**, p. 277); but the opposite was really true. The Labour members were swept into the House of Commons on a tidal wave of Liberalism that gave the party 377 seats and a majority of eighty-four over all other parties combined (**10**). Nevertheless, Balfour was not far wrong in seeing something especially significant about the results of the 1906 election. For, partly as a result of the MacDonald—Gladstone agreement, the L.R.C. now had an independent political power of its own; and this was indicated by its members sitting on the opposition benches when Parliament reassembled on 12 February 1906, and electing their own officers and Whips. On that day the thirty members of the parliamentary group (one new member had joined after the election) decided that they would adopt the simple title of — the Labour Party. A new parliamentary party had been born.

PART TWO

The Struggle for Power

3 The Growth of the Labour Party

LABOUR IN THE LIBERAL ERA, 1906-14

The infant Labour Party of 1906 was, as fundamentally it still is, a coalition of committed socialists and affiliated trade unionists. This characteristic was reflected in the Parliamentary Labour Party itself, where out of the thirty members only eighteen were socialists; and this cleavage between the two wings of the party came out clearly in the appointment of officials. Keir Hardie was elected Chairman of the party by only one vote, against David Shackleton of the Cotton Workers, the trade unionists' candidate; this was really a personal tribute to Hardie. Shackleton then became Vice-Chairman, Ramsay MacDonald was appointed Secretary, and Arthur Henderson Chief Whip. To maintain 'democracy' in the Parliamentary Party the Chairman was elected annually, and Hardie retained this post until 1907; though this was only 'a sentimental gesture', for he was never an outstanding parliamentarian. Henderson, who was acceptable to both socialists and trade unionists, succeeded him in 1908, and remained in office until, in 1910, he in turn was succeeded by George Barnes. Ramsay MacDonald became Chairman in 1911, and was re-elected annually until his resignation on the outbreak of war in 1914. It was MacDonald, much more so than his predecessors, who acted as *de facto* leader of the Parliamentary Party.

The socialists, particularly MacDonald and Philip Snowden, the fiery member for Blackburn, soon emerged as the most formidable and intelligent leaders of the Labour group; though, in the first few years at least, Shackleton was an important figure both because of his official links with the score or so trade union members outside the Labour Party, and because of his successful parliamentary campaign in favour of the T.U.C.'s Trade Union Bill. In fact 1906 was the most successful year for Labour in the history of the Liberal administration. Partly due to the especial sympathy of the Prime Minister, Henry Campbell-Bannerman, and the electoral commitments of many Liberal members, the Government threw overboard its own more moderate and complicated Trade Union Bill and accepted the Labour Bill. This involved, simply, a return to the *status quo* before Taff Vale as far as the legal liability of trade unions was concerned, and, in addition, the acceptance of the trade unionists' view of 'peaceful picketing'. Since the Conservative Party, for strictly opportunist reasons, had no wish to antagonise organised labour, the Bill became law as the Trades Disputes Act 1906. This was a major triumph for the Labour group; and in the same year they supported (and improved) a new Workmen's Compensation Act, and School Meals and Medical Inspection Acts.

This legislation, however, cut little ice with many Labour Party members. The next two years, moreover, due to the cautious and circumspect attitude of Asquith (who succeeded Campbell-Bannerman as Prime Minister in 1908) and the obstructionist tactics of the House of Lords, were particularly barren for labour. In 1908, the Eight-Hour Act was at last passed on behalf of the miners, though it belied its name; and in the same year the government approved a miserly Old Age Pensions scheme: five shillings a week at the age of seventy, if other sources of income were below ten shillings. Far more worrying for labour was the growing problem of unemployment. Ramsay MacDonald's 'Right to Work' Bill, which would have made it compulsory for local authorities to provide work for the unemployed, was rejected. All that John Burns did at the Local Government Board was to increase the 'hand-outs' to the local Distress Committees, and persist in his stone-walling opposition to any fundamental reform of the old Poor Law system.

The fate of MacDonald's Bill came to typify the relationship between the Liberal and Labour parties for the next six years. Never again after the initial success of the Trades Disputes Bill was the Labour Party able to impose its will on the Liberal Party; indeed, the opposite was true. The nature and pace of legislation were thereafter determined by the Liberal Ministers, and the members of the Parliamentary Labour Party often seemed to exist merely to provide voting fodder in support of Liberal issues — Lords' reform, Irish Home Rule, National Insurance — which they had not chosen and to which they gave no high priority. By 1910, as Keir Hardie said bitterly, the Labour Party had 'almost ceased to count', and disunity and disillusionment were gradually sapping the will of both leadership and rank and file. 'One lesson at any rate, can be enforced from the parliamentary work of the past eighteen months', the Parliamentary Committee had reported to the T.U.C. in 1907, 'and that is the political power that lies in the hands of labour' (**104**, p. 303). Yet, given that political power, why was the Labour Party during this period unable to emerge as a truly independent force within Parliament, with its own distinctive policies?

Some of the trouble lay with the composition of the Parliamentary

Labour Party itself. Apart from a few outstanding men like Hardie, MacDonald, Snowden, Shackleton and Henderson, the bulk of the Labour Party members represented, in Hyndman's phrase, 'A dull and deferential respectability'. Small in numbers, hampered by financial stringency and the pressures of trade union business, often ill-at-ease and inarticulate in Parliament and ignorant of or uninterested in the wider questions of debate, they made little impact on the House of Commons. The influence of the Party was in any case lessened by non-attendance of members, and indiscipline, the result, partly, of the notorious 'conscience clause', and, more fundamentally, the difficulties involved in the uneasy yoking together of trade unionists, still basically Lib-Lab in outlook, and socialists. Moreover, the socialists themselves were often bitterly divided over issues like National Insurance and the militant Suffragette Campaign. Nor had the Parliamentary Labour Party very much to offer by way of detailed specific proposals for reform; indeed, its initial reaction to many of the most famous of the Liberal measures was one of caution and suspicion. Thus, once the Liberals had paid their debts to their Labour allies by the legislation of 1906-08, the lead in social reform was soon taken over by the brilliant duumvirate, Lloyd George and Winston Churchill, the new Chancellor of the Exchequer and President of the Board of Trade; partly out of a genuine sympathy with the underdog, but also to revivify the Liberal Party and spike the guns of the socialists (51). 'The plain fact is', wrote Beatrice Webb, 'that Lloyd George and the Radicals have out-trumped the Labour Party' (115, p. 8). The Liberal programme of social legislation — trade boards, labour exchanges, national insurance — placed the Labour members in an unenviable situation. Such policies could not be rejected outright without them losing their credibility as members of a *Labour* Party, even though many of the socialists, Snowden and Lansbury in particular, objected strongly to important aspects of the legislation, such as the contributory principle in the Insurance Acts. On the other hand, their support for the Liberal Bills only underlined the absence of any viable Labour alternatives, and at the same time tied the Labour Party ever more closely to the Liberal Party. The skill, for example, with which Lloyd George not only destroyed the initial trade union suspicions of his National Health Insurance Bill but, through their role as 'Affiliated Societies', actually incorporated them in the administration of the Act, was a political victory of the highest order; but, as Halévy points out, it was 'first and foremost a victory over the new Labour party' (13, vi, 362).

It was not only the bait of social reform that made the Labour Party dance to the Liberals' tune during these years. The accession of the miners' group of M.P.s in 1909 tended to exacerbate the Lib-Lab tendencies of the Party. And, at the end of the same year the House of Lords decided in another explosive trade union decision, the Osborne Judgment, that it was illegal for a trade union to contribute financially to a political party. This struck a grave blow at the financial resources of the Labour Party, on the eve of a general election, and therefore (as with the Taff Vale decision) made the party look once again towards the Liberals for legislative redress. Unhappily for the Labour Party the situation now was very different from what it was in 1906. Partly because of the unprecedented behaviour of the Lords in rejecting the 'People's Budget' of 1909, the Liberals now had their own parliamentary priorities: two general elections in 1910, then the Parliament and Insurance Acts of 1911, followed by the Irish Home Rule and Welsh Disestablishment Bills of 1912. Thus the Labour Party found itself at the end of a long queue; and, though the Government introduced the 'Payment of Members' in 1911, as a *quid pro quo* for support for the Insurance Acts, they had to wait until 1913 before a new Trade Union Act in effect repealed the Osborne Judgment and restored the financial links between the trade unions and the Labour Party. In any case the political fortunes of the Liberal Party changed dramatically in 1910. For as a result of the two general elections of that year, the enormous Liberal majority of 1906 was cut down by about a quarter, thus making the two major parties in the House of Commons roughly equal in size. This meant that, in order to remain in office, the Liberal Party was absolutely dependent upon the Irish and Labour members; and, since the Labour Party (partly for financial reasons) had no wish to face a third general election, it felt itself impelled under these circumstances to keep the Liberals in office, vote for their Bills, and accept what crumbs they had to offer. Not that much was forthcoming for Labour in these last three years of peace: years of declining real income for the working class, bitter industrial and domestic strife, and wars and rumours of wars abroad. As Roy Jenkins writes: 'In retrospect 1911 shines out as the last year of Liberal achievement. Thereafter the seeds of disunity and decay found fertile soil in which to settle' (**16**, p. 187).

Yet for most contemporaries, including even many members of the Labour Party itself, it was their party and not the Liberals' that appeared to be 'strangely dying' during these years. For if, in terms of policy, the Labour Party acted only as a radical tail to the Liberal Party, electorally too it appeared to be making little headway. Between 1906 and 1910 the number of members of the Parliamentary Labour Party rose from thirty to forty-five, owing primarily to the accession of the miners' M.P.s in 1909. In the general election of January 1910, seventy-eight Labour candidates stood and, thanks to the tacit continuance of the electoral pact, only twenty-six were opposed by official Liberal candidates. Forty Labour men were successful, but not one of these had been opposed by an official Liberal! In the December election of that year, the Labour Party only put forward fifty-six candidates. Forty-two were elected but, once again, only two were successful in opposition to official Liberal candidates, one of them being George Lansbury at Bow. The final outcome of the 1910 elections, therefore, was to reduce the total number of Labour M.P.s from forty-five to forty-two; and, through by-election losses, this total was down to thirty-six on the eve of the First World War. Even electorally, therefore, during these prewar years, the Labour Party was unable to break away from the gravitational pull of the Liberal Party. 'There was nothing here to quieten the mounting criticism of the militants within the party and the unions, and nothing to rekindle the movement's waning political enthusiasm and purpose' (84, p. 422).

As early as 1907 there was a growing disillusionment among many rank-and-file members with the official leadership of the party; for, despite the great triumph of 1906, and the social legislation of the Liberals, the lot of the working classes seemed to deteriorate rather than improve, and indeed we know that real wages declined by at least ten per cent in the first decade of the twentieth century (15). 'It is necessary to make it perfectly clear', wrote Ramsay MacDonald in a private letter, '. . . that the Labour Party is not the Liberal Party in order to keep the movement together. That is all I have been doing. At the same time I have been stating that much of the Liberal legislation has been excellent' (120, p. 147). Many socialists would have argued that not only was the latter statement untrue, but that MacDonald's truckling to the Liberal Party contradicted his own aim of 'independence'. This was roughly the argument of Ben Tillett's pamphlet of 1908, *Is the Parliamentary Labour Party a Failure?* [doc. 17a] ; and even the Parliamentary Committee of the T.U.C. emphasised in 1910 that 'from the legislative point of view Labour has so far gained little' (84, p. 405). This growing militancy was seen expressed in 1907 in Pete Curran's victory over a Liberal at the Jarrow by-election; and, even more significantly, in the victory of Victor Grayson, standing as an independent socialist, at Colne Valley. 'Organised Socialism has risen up in the night', commented the *Daily Telegraph* on the latter's victory; and sympathy with Grayson was so marked at the I.L.P. Annual Conference in 1907 that MacDonald, Hardie, Snowden and Glasier resigned from the Council in protest. Yet his victory was something of a flash in the pan; and both Colne Valley and Jarrow reverted to the Liberals at the general election of January 1910 (**26**, ch. 8). Grayson and his socialist supporters then began campaigning for an end to the 'Labour Alliance'; and this led to the foundation in 1911, as the result of a union between the Social Democratic Party (as the old S.D.F. now called itself) and a number of militant I.L.P. branches, of the British Socialist Party, forerunner of the Communist Party of Great Britain. Indeed, new socialist societies sprang up like mushrooms overnight during these prewar years: the Scottish Socialist Labour Party had been formed by a group of dissident S.D.F. members as early as 1903, and this was to achieve fame later as the basis of the 'Clydesiders' party (**95**).

These 'revolutionary' movements within the socialist camp seemed to contemporaries (and to many historians) to link up with the 'Syndicalist' movement in trade unionism which, drawing on French and American theory and practice, was spread in this country by Tom Mann particularly, after he returned from Australia in 1910 (**105**). The so-called 'Labour Unrest' of 1911-14 seemed a tribute to the potency of Syndicalist ideas. This unrest was marked by major industrial disputes on the railways and in the docks and mines; attempts to form 'industrial' unions; and the formation in 1914 of the famous 'Triple Alliance' between the Transport Workers, Miners and Railwaymen to coordinate wage demands. Syndicalism could be seen, therefore, both as a reaction against conservative trade union leadership, and as a movement in support of the principle of 'direct action' in opposition to the total commitment to parliamentary action of the Labour Party leaders. From every point of view, therefore, the Labour Party during these pre-war years seemed to be in a desperately weak position [**doc. 17b**] . 'The end of this period, accordingly', writes Carl Brand, 'found the Labour party dependent upon the Liberals, dissatisfied with its achievement, unsure of its aims, and apparently in decline' (**56**, p. 28).

But there is much to be said on the other side. As far as the Syndicalist movement is concerned, it is clear that this affected only a tiny minority of workers; and the 'Labour Unrest' of 1911-14, as Pelling and other historians have stressed, was concerned more with traditional demands for union recognition and better wages and conditions of work, than with ideologies (**26**, ch. 9; **104**). It is true that there was some success for the syndicalist concept of 'industrial' unionism and 'direct action' during these years, with the formation of the Transport Workers' Federation in 1910, the National Union of Railwaymen in 1913, and the 'Triple Alliance' in the following year. But neither of these new amalgamations embraced all the workers within their particular industries: A.S.L.E.F. and the Railway Clerks' Association are still with us, and 'Black Friday', 15 April 1921, was to show what a thing of clay was the Triple Alliance! Indeed, once again, as with new unionism in the later nineteenth century, it was the slow unpublicised development of orthodox trade unionism that was far more important. By 1911 there were 1,661,000 trade unionists in the country: by 1913 this figure had leapt to 2,682,000 − a sixty per cent increase in two years! This expansion was partly due to the association of the trade unions with the new National Insurance schemes of Lloyd George; and therefore, as Halévy says: 'We are driven to the paradoxical conclusion that during those very years in which revolutionary syndicalism was so vocal, cooperation between the trade unions and the Government became closer than before' (**13**, vi, 479).

The left-wing socialist revolt against the 'Labour Alliance' similarly was, and remained, a minority movement. Both Ramsay MacDonald and Keir Hardie firmly opposed any attempt by the I.L.P. to break with their trade union allies in the Labour Party; and, despite the sympathy shown to Grayson at the 1907 Congress of the party, in the following year the I.L.P. threw out by an overwhelming majority a resolution to disaffiliate from the Labour Party. Within the Labour Party itself, the overwhelming influence of the big union battalions of coal and cotton, and the personal ascendancy of MacDonald meant, as even Beatrice Webb regretfully acknowledged, that there was no real challenge to the cautious moderate line pursued by the party leadership which indeed had much to commend it (**71**). Electorally too, though the Labour Party made little progress between 1906 and 1914, the conditions were being prepared nationally for the great leap forward that the party was able to make in the postwar world. Labour membership of local bodies more than doubled during this period, often at the expense of the Liberals, as did affiliations to the parent party from trades councils and local labour parties; the foundation of the London Labour Party in 1914, for example, was a major event in the party's history. The *Daily Herald*, founded in 1911 by George Lansbury, soon became an outstanding newspaper; while the writings of the Syndicalists and Guild Socialists, in particular, showed the vigour and pungency of the continuing debate on the nature and aims of the Labour Movement.

But, above all, it was the increasing support from the trade unions that was of key importance. Trade union affiliations between 1906 and 1914 increased from 904,496 to 1,572,391; and here the accession of the miners in 1909 was of particular significance. Their conversion from Liberalism to the Labour Party was due not only to increasing quarrels with the coalowners (often Liberals) over wages and conditions of work, but also to the spread of socialist ideas among the younger generation of union leaders. This belated *volte face* was, as Dr Gregory has shown in detail, 'a major political event' (**90**). For the miners controlled, potentially, about ninety parliamentary seats; and though before 1914 Liberals sat for fifty-nine of them, once the electoral pact between the Liberal/Labour leaders broke down, as it was rapidly doing at constituency level in 1914, changing social and economic conditions were likely to sweep them into the Labour net. This is exactly what did happen during the decade after 1918; and what was true for the mining constituencies was true also for other major industrial seats. The Parliamentary Labour Party may have been small during these years, but it was its growing extraparliamentary support among the trade unions, so important in terms of membership, morale and finance, that was to be of decisive importance for the future (**26**, ch. 6).

THE FIRST WORLD WAR AND ITS AFTERMATH

The First World War had a dramatic effect on the fortunes of the British political parties. As a result of the writings of recent historians we now know in detail the story of how the Liberal Party, divided after 1916 between Asquith and Lloyd George, tore itself to pieces during the war and emerged in 1918 as 'a weak, disunited minority party (**30**, **31**). It is often forgotten, however, that the Labour Party too was divided over the war, yet it emerged at the end of the conflict united and confident, with its organisation remodelled, and committed to a definite party programme. With the fate of the Liberal Party in our minds, it is important to consider the reasons for this.

The British Labour Party, like practically everyone else in the country, was caught unawares by the outbreak of war on the Continent in the summer of 1914. At first, in the spirit of the famous resolution of the Stuttgart Congress of the Second International in 1907, the party opposed intervention; but following the German invasion of Belgium on 4 August the bulk of the party swung strongly in support of Britain's declaration of war against Germany. The Labour Party Executive, however, still remained very critical of prewar policies which, they believed, had helped to produce the war; and on 5 August they passed a resolution asserting 'that its duty is now to secure peace at the earliest possible moment on such conditions as will produce the best opportunities for the re-establishment of amicable feelings between the workers of Europe' (**60**, p. 18).

In its support for the war effort the Executive was strongly backed by the Fabians, and even a section of the Social Democrats led by

Hyndman. But the I.L.P., with its pacifist tradition and profound belief in the 'imperialist' causes of the war, adopted a firm antiwar attitude, as did all its parliamentary members. As a result, Ramsay MacDonald resigned as Chairman of the Parliamentary Party and was succeeded by Arthur Henderson. The break between the pro- and antiwar sections of the Labour Party, however, partly due to the tact and patience of Henderson, did not become a wide and irreconcilable gulf. There was never, therefore, the deep personal bitterness that marked the two sections of the Liberal Party after the schism of 1916; and in any case, once hostilities commenced, the practical differences between the two sides were not all that great. 'We condemn the policy which has produced the war, we do not obstruct the war effort, but our duty is to secure peace at the earliest possible moment', wrote MacDonald (**120**, p. 248), though his colleagues, notably Snowden, were not quite so conciliatory. Moreover, the federal structure of the Labour Party allowed MacDonald to retain his seat on the Labour Party Executive as an I.L.P. member; and both prowar and antiwar sections could work together over social questions.

The conditions of modern warfare meant that the direct cooperation of the trade unions was vital, and from this simple fact organised labour could and did in the long run gain enormously in power and prestige. In the short run, however, the unions had to make sacrifices; and, following the 'electoral truce' agreed to on the outbreak of war, the T.U.C. agreed voluntarily to abandon for the duration the use of the strike weapon and restrictive practices, and to accept 'dilution' of labour and compulsory arbitration. These agreements were given the force of law by the Ministry of War Act in July 1915. By that time the Labour Party had accepted the logic of its support for the war and had entered the Government. The problem of whether or not to take office had caused some heart-searching in the party when, in May, owing to criticisms of his conduct of the war, Asquith had been forced to widen his government by inviting the Conservative and Labour parties to participate. Snowden, the sea-green incorruptible, for example, speaking on behalf of the I.L.P., argued that the party would lose its freedom of independent criticism if it joined a Government dominated by Conservatives and Liberals. In the end, however, the Party Conference approved the Executive's decision to accept Asquith's offer, and Arthur Henderson joined the Government, ostensibly in a ministerial position, but in reality as adviser on labour problems.

This meant that, as Snowden had foretold, Labour was now committed to public support for the less palatable decisions of the coalition: opposition to the left-wing agitation on Clydeside and in South

Wales over industrial grievances and rising prices, and, in 1916, support for conscription. The Labour Party Conference of 1916 was strongly patriotic, endorsing these decisions and shunning any direct contact — through the previous year's Zimmerwald Conference of neutral socialists — with their German counterparts. These attitudes made it fairly certain that, despite their personal regard for Asquith and ignorance of the machinations that brought about his downfall, Labour would feel impelled to follow the more dynamic, and indeed more pro-Labour, leadership of Lloyd George when he assumed power in December 1916.

The support of Labour was a great triumph for Lloyd George, and without it his position as Prime Minister would have been untenable. But Labour gained much in return. Henderson was promoted to membership of the Inner War Cabinet of five, and other Labour men were given a number of ministerial posts. Furthermore, Lloyd George was now committed to a number of 'collectivist' measures, such as food rationing, state control of mines, shipping etc., which had been demanded by that year's Party Conference (**19**). Labour's support for the new Government was therefore endorsed by an overwhelming majority at the Party Conference in the following year. These events were of decisive importance for the Labour Party. At last it was freed from the accusation of being tied to the coat tails of the Liberal Party — the bulk of whose supporters, led by Asquith, were now in opposition — and its members were equal partners in a Coalition Government headed by Lloyd George. Yet, paradoxically, the Labour Party still retained its independence, both in terms of past responsibilities and its own future policies. 'But in the long run', as Trevor Wilson writes, 'it was to prove an advantage that, unlike the Liberals, Labour was not directly responsible for the alleged errors or misdeeds of the past' (**31**, p. 30).

One other result of Labour's support for Lloyd George was to widen the split between the pro- and antiwar sections of the party, and indeed Philip Snowden's opposition speech at the 1916 Party Conference was one of his bitterest, and most unrealistic, efforts. Yet within eighteen months the gulf between the two sides was rapidly narrowing. This was the result of the dramatic events of 1917 — one of the decisive dates in modern history. For in March of that year the war-weary Russian people rose in revolt and overthrew the Tsarist autocracy. A liberal Provisional Government was then established whose socialist members demanded a negotiated peace based on 'no annexations or indemnities'. These world-shattering events had a profound effect on the inchoate demands for 'a just peace' already developing within the British Left. One result of the Russian revolution, therefore, was to stimulate the antiwar and extreme socialist groups in Britain into renewed activity; and this led to the 'leftist' Leeds Congress of June 1917, attended by an embarrassed Ramsay MacDonald, which proved a resounding failure. Much more important was the fact that the prowar moderates within the Labour Party now began to move to the left; and the key figure here was that pillar of respectability and member of the War Cabinet, Arthur Henderson.

For in the spring of 1917 the neutral socialists planned a conference at Stockholm of *all* belligerent socialist groups to discuss peace terms; soon afterwards Kerensky came to power in Russia, to be followed by the failure of the Russian spring offensive. The British Government now arranged to send Henderson on a war mission to Russia, and there he came to the conclusion that the Stockholm Conference *should* be supported. Lloyd George refused him a visa to go. He therefore justified his position in a remarkable speech to a special Labour Party Conference on 10 August 1917, and was received with acclamation (5, pp. 222-9). The following day he resigned (to be replaced by George Barnes) and thus automatically resumed his position as Secretary of the Labour Party and leader of the parliamentary group, though he soon relinquished the latter office. In the event the Stockholm Conference, which proved abortive, turned out to be much less important than Henderson's resignation. For, freed from office, Arthur Henderson was able to concentrate on the reorganisation of the Labour Party and the formulation of its ideas on foreign policy, a programme which brought him into close contact with Ramsay MacDonald and the antiwar group and thus paved the way for that postwar reconciliation within the party that was to be one of his greatest achievements. In the second half of 1917, therefore, with one foot still in the Government, the Labour Party, as the American Ambassador observed, was already 'playing for supremacy' (74, p. 42).

Under the inspiration of Henderson the Labour Party began to develop a detailed programme for a 'just peace', a programme in which Henderson worked closely with MacDonald and Sidney Webb, and received the tacit support of the T.U.C. Their eventual statement of War Aims — embodying the classical radical demands for a League of Nations, open diplomacy, disarmament etc. — was strongly supported by a special Party Conference which met in December 1917 [doc. 18]. Indeed, Labour's seizure of the initiative in formulating these ideas led Lloyd George, at last, to make general moves in the same direction, and anticipated in spirit Wilson's Fourteen Points, proclaimed on 8 January 1918. Labour was now far ahead of the other parties in thinking seriously and constructively about the future peace settlement: and this did much to raise its prestige in the eyes of those disillusioned members of the Liberal Left, associated with the Union of Democratic Control (29), who began to see in the Labour Party (in the words of *The Nation*) 'the one quarter from which a really fresh and hopeful development can come' (31, p. 139).

The other part of Henderson's work was his attempt to establish an efficient national organisation and a clearcut programme for the Labour Party, so that when the time came it would be in a position to capture the votes of those millions of men and women who would be enfranchised by the Parliament Act of 1918. At the outbreak of war in 1914 the Labour Party was not a national party. It had few individual members, and was really a federal organisation, membership of which was based on affiliations through trade unions (numbering nearly two million) and the socialist societies (only some 30,000 to 40,000). This structure meant that there was no sort of labour electoral organisation in the majority of constituencies; where there was it depended for its existence on the support of local Trades and Labour Councils, Miners' Lodges and, above all, the Independent Labour Party which, with its 672 branches, formed easily the most vigorous and enthusiastic part of the grass-roots labour movement (88). Labour had therefore never put up more than seventy-eight candidates at a general election, a figure which could now be regarded, rightly, as derisory.

In his plans for a new constitution for the Labour Party, in which he again worked closely with Webb and MacDonald, Henderson aimed at grafting on to the federal structure a nationwide network of local constituency parties. He proposed, therefore, to convert the local 'scratch' organisations into local Labour Party branches, in which, in order to appeal to non-unionists and middle-class people, individual membership would be encouraged; affiliated trade unions were also to pay increased fees. In addition, a new Party Executive of twenty-one members was suggested, to be elected by the Annual Conference as a whole (thus enabling the unions to dominate it with their block votes), consisting of eleven members representing the trade unions and socialist societies, five the local labour parties, and four the women's organisations: the Party Treasurer was to be elected separately. Opposition was expected from the I.L.P., which under the new arrangements would lose its separate representation and be faced, moreover, with rivalry from the new local labour parties. In the end, however, the I.L.P., partly due to its belief in its own capacity for survival and growth, and partly due to the fact that 'Socialism' (even though the word was not mentioned) was written into the new Constitution in the famous Clause Four, did not oppose the new arrangements, and they were accepted by the Party Conference in February 1918 with only one important change — the addition of two extra representatives for the first group of the Executive [**doc. 19**] . Labour's programme was spelled out in more detail in Sidney Webb's *Labour and the New Social Order*, published in June 1918. This document was based on four main principles: (1) the idea of a 'national minimum'; (2) democratic control of industry (though the details were deliberately left vague); (3) financial reform; (4) surplus wealth to be employed for the common good. Its underlying ethos was thus distinctly Fabian, and it was Webb's programme, embodied in a series of detailed resolutions, that was accepted by the Labour Party in the same month. As Cole wrote in 1948: 'In Great Britain, for both good and ill, it charted the course on which the Labour Party has been set ever since' (**60**, p. 61).

The acceptance of the new Constitution and Programme was Labour's order of release; and in November, three days after the Armistice, the party decided to withdraw from the Coalition, though a few dissentients, like George Barnes, stayed on. A snap election was quickly arranged by Lloyd George for December — the famous 'Coupon Election', so called because selected candidates who supported the Coalition Government were given a letter of recommendation (or 'coupon') signed jointly by Lloyd George and Bonar Law, the Conservative leader. The Labour Party was not very well prepared for the coming contest: its new organisation was hardly off the drawing board. Nevertheless, it put up 361 candidates, an enormous increase compared with the seventy-eight of December 1910. The atmosphere of the election, with its facile slogans and cheap patriotism, made it difficult for the opposition parties to present their case, and Lloyd George and his supporters won an overwhelming victory. Even so, the Labour Party secured fifty-seven seats and gained more than two million votes (compared with forty-two seats and under half a million votes in December 1910). Unfortunately, the new Parliamentary Party was all tail and no head; for its best leaders — MacDonald, Snowden and Henderson — lost their seats, and only J. R. Clynes survived from the first rank to become *de facto* leader of the parliamentary group.

In the immediate postwar years, therefore, 'parliamentary socialism' seemed to have been emasculated; a position which was emphasised by the increase of political militancy, exemplified by the foundation of the British Communist Party in 1920, and the dramatic events in the industrial field (**98**). For organised labour, revelling in its freedom from wartime restrictions and conscious of its enhanced power, was determined to maintain its recent wage gains, and even, as in the famous incident of the 'Jolly George', to use 'direct action' to influence the

Government's foreign policy. Hence the year 1919 was marked by a rash of strikes and rumours of strikes. By the end of the year, however, the revolutionary edge had been taken off the workers' agitation by the rapid increases in wages that accompanied the postwar boom until, in the summer of 1920, the bubble burst, and the mounting unemployment (soon nearly two million) and the beginning of a counterattack by the employers, produced another wave of industrial strife (23, 94). This time it was the miners, always at the storm centre of labour unrest throughout the interwar period, who took the lead. Betrayed, as they believed, by the Government's rejection of the Sankey Commission's Report in favour of nationalisation of the mines in 1919, and determined to resist the mineowners' demand for wage cuts, they decided on strike action, and summoned to their aid their prewar allies of the 'Triple Alliance'. But on 'Black Friday', 15 April 1921, the miners found themselves deserted by the dockers and railwaymen and left to struggle on by themselves until June, when they were forced to return to work, virtually on the owners' terms. 'Black Friday', writes Taylor, 'marked . . . a clash between two conceptions of union policy – the old outlook of class war, to be fought with the bullheaded obstinacy of the trenches, and a new unionism, aiming at compromise or even partnership' (30, p. 146). Militancy faded away in a general round of wage cuts, union recrimination, and detestation of Lloyd George. The real beneficiaries of these events were, therefore, the established leaders of the trade unions and the Labour Party.

For the weakness of the Labour Party during these years was more apparent than real. It is true that in the actual number of its parliamentary members it had not improved markedly over its prewar record; but the circumstances of 1918, with a 'snap' election, a new electorate and a low poll, helped to explain this. It had, however, obtained some two-and-a-quarter million votes out of nearly eleven million cast; the Asquith Liberals obtained about half that number and ended up with only twenty-eight seats. What this meant, therefore, was that the prewar roles of the two parties were completely reversed: it was Labour now that seemed to be the official progressive party, while it was the Liberals who could justly be accused of splitting the 'radical' vote. After 1918 the Labour Party therefore had a sound bastion of strength, particularly in the industrial and mining districts, upon which, given the considerable advantages it now possessed, it could hope to build. For under the new Constitution, as Henderson had hoped, local Labour parties gradually spread until by 1924 there were only three constituencies which lacked one. Nor, in those early years, was there any marked rivalry with the I.L.P., which had shed its left-wing to the

Communist Party and still remained loyal to MacDonald; indeed, the years up to 1924 were the highwater mark of I.L.P. influence within the party (88, 68). The 'idealism' of Labour's foreign policy during these years, as well as the details of its party programme, also attracted middle- and upper-class men and women, like Clement Attlee and C. P. Trevelyan, many of them ex-Liberals, who were later to serve with distinction in the Labour Governments [doc. 20].

Important too was the growth and rationalisation of the trade union movement, from which the Labour Party inevitably gained in members, money and voting power, since for many trade unionists it was now becoming as normal to vote Labour as it had been for their fathers to vote Liberal. There were now more than six million trade unionists affiliated to the T.U.C. (and another two million outside), and many of these had recently been organised into new amalgamations, often under younger leaders like Ernest Bevin: the Iron and Steel Trades Confederation (1917); the Amalgamated Engineering Union (1920); and, biggest of all, Bevin's Transport and General Workers (1921). In recognition of these changed conditions the T.U.C., like the Labour Party, reorganised itself in 1921 by replacing its old Parliamentary Committee by a new General Council with wider powers. New links were then established with the Labour Party by setting up a National Joint Council which represented equally the General Council of the T.U.C., the National Executive of the Labour Party, and the Parliamentary Labour Party (83).

Nor could this Labour Establishment, despite the contentions of its enemies, be easily tarred with the Communist brush. It is true that the Labour Party was pro-Russian in the sense that, as Professor Graubard has shown, it was against military intervention to overthrow the Bolshevik regime and was in favour of giving diplomatic recognition to the new Soviet state (65). But, as Arthur Henderson pointed out continually to Labour Party Conferences, there were fundamental differences between British Socialism and Soviet Communism, and Lenin's insulting comments on British Labour leaders merely emphasised Henderson's arguments (103). Hence the British Labour Party, despite the successful communist seduction of other European socialist parties, would have no truck with the Third International, and it was indeed the main instigator and prop of the Second (Socialist) International, revived in 1923. Moreover, between 1920 and 1922 Labour Party Conferences rejected overwhelmingly three attempts by the recently formed British Communist Party to affiliate, and followed this up by tightening the regulations against the representation of Communist delegates in Labour Party affairs (98).

Thus in various ways an 'undogmatic Labourism' (in Pelling's phrase) was being built up among the industrial working class during these postwar years; and this could already be seen in Labour's considerable gains in local elections in 1919, and in its fourteen by-election victories between 1918 and 1922. The tendencies at work were apparent in the general election of 1922. This came about as a result of the famous 'Carlton Club' decision of the Conservative Party in October to repudiate Lloyd George and reassert their *de facto* supremacy. As a result Lloyd George resigned, and followed Asquith into opposition. He was succeeded by the Conservative leader, Bonar Law, who quickly held a general election in which his party won a notable victory. For Labour, the election of 1922 was significant for a number of reasons. In the first place it drove home what the previous six years seemed to imply: that the Liberals, even with Lloyd George and his followers in opposition, could still not impress themselves on the country as an alternative government. Labour, with 142 seats to the united Liberal total of 116 was now *the* alternative government to the Conservatives; and the Parliamentary Labour Party was in a better position than ever before to take advantage of that fact. Most of its old leaders were now back in the Commons, together with an important contingent of new members, including the famous 'Clydeside' group led by Maxton and Wheatley, twenty-nine strong (**101**). The party's greatest gains were in Scotland, where the I.L.P. was particularly powerful, Yorkshire, South Wales and London. Thus Labour was much more clearly a *national* party, not only geographically but also socially, since trade unionists now formed only half the parliamentary membership. Ironically, it was the Clydesiders' support that led to the election of Ramsay MacDonald as leader of the Parliamentary Party, a choice that was to make him within two years the first Labour Prime Minister.

THE FIRST LABOUR GOVERNMENT, 1924

A Labour Government so soon after the Conservative victory of 1922 was something which no one either inside or outside the Labour Party really expected, and indeed the circumstances in which Ramsay MacDonald became Prime Minister were almost unprecedented. In May 1923 Bonar Law, the Conservative Prime Minister, retired through ill-health and was succeeded by the Chancellor of the Exchequer, Stanley Baldwin. Baldwin came to the conclusion that the only solution for the grave problem of unemployment was a policy of protection. He decided, therefore, in accordance with his predecessor's undertaking, to obtain a 'mandate' from the electorate before embarking on such a policy, and accordingly Parliament was dissolved and a general election held in December. By making Tariff Reform the one real issue in their electoral campaign, the Conservative Party ensured the reunification of the Liberal Party under the leadership of Asquith (with Lloyd George acting as paymaster) to defend the sacred ark of Free Trade. The Labour Party too supported Free Trade, though its platform also contained a number of nebulous proposals for strengthening the League of Nations and dealing with unemployment, as well as a limited nationalisation programme. In effect, therefore, there were two elections fought in 1923: one between the Liberals and Conservatives over the well-worn issue of Free Trade, in which the Liberals won a number of seats, particularly in rural England (11); and another between the Liberals and the Labour Party for control of the 'industrial' vote, in which the latter made a moderate advance. The Labour Party polled about four and a quarter million votes (only slightly more than in 1922) and obtained 191 seats. The party's greatest gains were in the London area where the Labour members now numbered forty-six; the I.L.P. group in the Commons also rose significantly, thus reiterating the anti-trade union bias which had typified the previous Parliament. The Liberals polled nearly as many votes as Labour and obtained 158 seats; the Conservatives, with 258, still remained the largest party in the House of Commons.

But since the results of the 1923 election could be interpreted as a clear vote against Tariff Reform, the Liberal Party was now prepared to cooperate with its former rivals in ousting the Conservatives – which was done on 21 January 1924 – and allowing Labour to assume office. Asquith's motives were as usual a mixture of idealism and political calculation. He intended to use his commanding position in the Commons to keep a tight rein over the policies of any future Labour government, believing that, if such an experiment failed, power would devolve once more into his own welcoming and respectable hands. But would Ramsay MacDonald accept office under such conditions? There were many obvious arguments against acceptance. In the end the Labour leader was moved by two major considerations: he felt it would be cowardly to refuse the responsibility of carrying out some part at least of Labour's programme in domestic and, more especially, foreign affairs – a refusal which would be bound to play into the hands of Asquith and Lloyd George. He felt too, as did his colleagues, that whatever the final outcome of a minority Labour administration, the party would at least gain experience of government. 'One step!', he said in a speech at Hull, '. . . on one condition that it leads to the next step. If we shirk our responsibilities now we should inflict upon ourselves the defeat that our enemies could not inflict upon us' (**67**, p. 93). On 22 January 1924, therefore, Ramsay MacDonald decided to accept office as head of the first Labour Government, a decision that was greeted with enormous enthusiasm by the party. 'Today 23 years ago', wrote King George V in his diary, 'dear Grandmama died. I wonder what she would have thought of a Labour Government!' (**130**, p. 497).

In 1924 Ramsay MacDonald seemed pre-eminently fitted to become the first Labour Prime Minister. Handsome, dignified, intelligent, possessed of a magnificent voice which made him an impressive speaker both inside and outside the House of Commons, he was, in Shinwell's phrase, 'a prince among men'. Unlike Henderson, for example, he had had no ministerial experience; but ever since his appointment as Secretary of the Labour Representation Committee in 1900 he had served in a variety of administrative posts within the Labour movement, which brought him into touch, directly or indirectly, with every important section of its work, and his skill as a negotiator was widely acknowledged. But MacDonald was not just a committee-man. He had a greater knowledge of foreign countries and foreign affairs than the average Labour member; he had also written widely on socialism and labour questions and, as an active journalist, he still contributed a weekly column to the I.L.P. paper *Forward*. Moreover, though he was clearly a 'moderate' in Labour Party terms, as his writings and speeches proved irrefutably, the left-wingers within the party, by a curious optical illusion, were still able to see MacDonald as one of themselves, partly because of his antiwar record and his special associations with the I.L.P. It is true that his thinking about economics and politics lacked incisiveness, and that his conception of socialism was vague and emotional. But in all this he personified the movement that he led (**68**).

The difficulties that faced him as Prime Minister in 1924 were formidable. In the first place there was the immediate problem of forming a Cabinet: few of his colleagues had much administrative experience, and MacDonald's opinion of their abilities was in any case rather low. In the end, partly by going outside the Labour ranks to fill 'technical' posts such as the Admiralty, and giving office to ex-Liberals like Trevelyan and Haldane, he solved the problem with considerable skill. MacDonald himself, unwisely as it turned out, combined the Foreign Office with the premiership; Snowden became the Chancellor of the Exchequer; Arthur Henderson went to the Home Office; and a 'Clydesider', John Wheatley, became Minister of Health [**doc. 21a**]. The fact, however, that only one left-winger was given a major post in the Government — Lansbury was conspicuous by his absence — meant that the left-wing element in the party, resentful in any case of their dependence on the Liberals, became increasingly restive. The other great problem facing MacDonald stemmed indeed from the fact that he headed a minority Government dependent on Liberal support. Neither the Labour leaders nor the Labour rank-and-file were grateful for this prop; rather they were incensed that the Liberal Party had the indecency to go on living. They rejected utterly any notion of a coalition with the Liberals, and while in office remained as hostile and contemptuous of them as before – an attitude that in the end was to bring about their downfall. 'Liberals', said Lloyd George bitterly, 'are to be the oxen to drag the Labour wain over the rough roads of Parliament for two or three years, goaded along, and at the end of the journey, when there is no further use for them, they are to be slaughtered. That is the Labour idea of cooperation' (**67**, pp. 235-6). Nevertheless, the new Government *was* forced to accept the fact that, as the price of their uneasy cooperation with the Liberals, socialistic schemes were ruled out – a prospect that was not perhaps altogether displeasing to the Prime Minister.

Hence the Labour Government's achievement in the domestic field, partly, though not entirely, due to that fact, was limited and largely negative. Much was done to destroy the cheese-paring economies introduced by the 'Geddes Axe', particularly in the field of education, where C. P. Trevelyan proved a capable and progressive Minister. The one great positive achievement on the domestic front was Wheatley's Housing Act which, by a policy of increased subsidies to the local authorities coupled with special agreements with the builders' unions, began a building programme which in the course of the next decade made half a million new houses available for rent to working-class families. Something was also done to improve the conditions for the payment of unemployment benefit; but the major problem of *curing* unemployment proved to be more intractable. The task was not helped by the attitude of the new Chancellor. Snowden's Budget was a paean to the glories of Free Trade; and his Gladstonian rectitude at the Treasury (though its defects were not appreciated at the time) made it difficult to embark on unorthodox or costly schemes for dealing with unemployment. The Labour Party seemed hypnotised by the belief that in the long run with the introduction of socialism the problem of unemployment would disappear. In the short run, however, apart from paying lip-service to the notion of public works, which were both costly and slow to take effect, it was rather helpless before the complexities of the problem. Over unemployment the party leadership in 1924 was timid, unconstructive and muddled in its thinking, though in this it was partly the victim of the conventional economic wisdom of the time.

The seeds were already being sown for the disaster that was to overtake it in 1931 [doc. 21b].

In foreign affairs, on the other hand, the Labour Government's record is generally considered to be much better, though its achievements, as Professor Winkler has argued, marked a fairly decisive break with the party's views in the immediate postwar years (82). For, after 1918, Labour's attitude towards foreign affairs was still strongly influenced by the pacifism and muddled Marxism of the I.L.P. This meant hostility to France and her obsession with 'security', typified by the French occupation of the Ruhr in 1922; opposition to the 'injustices' of Versailles, and therefore sympathy with Germany; and suspicions of the League of Nations as an alliance of capitalist states. By 1922, however, due primarily to the efforts of Henderson and Clynes, the Labour Party leadership began to adopt a more realistic assessment of the international situation, and particularly of the League. When he assumed office in 1924 MacDonald was able to push this new approach a little farther, and carve out for himself a role as 'mediator' in European affairs. As a result of his policy of cooperation with France, particularly through negotiations with the moderate Herriot, his opposite number, MacDonald was able to obtain a final French withdrawal from the Ruhr. Then, as a result of the London Conference, over which he presided, he obtained their support for the Dawes Plan, a short-term solution of the reparations problem based on international loans to Germany. 'We sign it', said the British Prime Minister, 'with a feeling that we have turned our backs on the terrible years of war and war mentality'. It was, comments Professor Lyman, 'the high point of MacDonald's career' (67, p. 164). This agreement was to be but a preliminary step to the achievement of general European security; and for this MacDonald and other League statesmen pinned their hopes on disarmament coupled with a widening of the League's powers to deal with international disputes. The outcome of this approach was the Geneva Protocol of 1924; but, owing to the nature of the commitments that it specified, it is doubtful if in the end the Labour Government would have signed it, and it was in any case repudiated by the next Conservative Ministry.

These policies, whether they are to be regarded as successes or failures, were relatively uncontroversial. This was not true of MacDonald's attempts to restore more normal relations with the Bolshevik Government of Russia. Here, though his motives were commendable, his methods were remarkably clumsy. Diplomatic recognition of the Soviet Government was granted soon after Labour came to power; and this was followed by an Anglo-Russian Conference in

August which aimed at settling the outstanding differences between the two countries and embodying them in formal Anglo-Soviet treaties. The most controversial proposal was that of a British loan to Russia, to be linked with a vague Soviet agreement to provide compensation for British bondholders whose claims had been wiped out during the Revolution. As Sidney Webb suggested, the proposal was 'electorally calamitous' since it meant that the Labour Government could be branded as pro-Communist, despite the mass of evidence to the contrary (81). It thus played into the hands of the Conservative opposition — and Lloyd George.

The Liberal leader, whose patience was wearing thin under the continual insults of the Labour members, was now prepared to use the pretext of the proposed Anglo-Soviet treaties to unite with the Conservatives in order to bring about the downfall of the Labour Government. Most Liberals were prepared to follow Lloyd George's lead, since they were strongly against the idea of a loan to Russia, and were convinced that this had only been agreed to as a result of pressure on the government from the Labour left-wingers; and indeed it was true that after they had broken down completely at one point, Anglo-Russian discussions were only resumed as a result of their intervention. It was, therefore, their Russian policy that was the real cause of the Labour Government's downfall. The actual occasion, however, was the famous 'Campbell Case' which arose out of the proposed governmental prosecution of J. R. Campbell, a leading Communist, for seditious writing. This case was badly handled by the Prime Minister and Sir Patrick Hastings, the Attorney-General, and as a result Liberals and Conservatives combined together to defeat the Government on what had been made a vote of confidence. MacDonald resigned, Parliament was dissolved, and a general election was held in October.

That election has achieved a certain notoriety by the publication in the middle of the campaign of the so-called 'Zinoviev Letter' [doc. 22]. Due to its timing, its substance, and the inept way in which it was handled by the Prime Minister, it provided a golden opportunity for the Conservative propaganda machine and thus, so it has been argued, brought about Labour's defeat. It is true that the Conservatives easily won the election: in a heavy poll they obtained about two million more votes than in 1923, and gained 419 seats. But Labour also increased its vote, and though it lost forty seats it still returned 151 members. The real losers in the election of 1924 were the Liberals, whose poll slumped badly and whose members declined from 158 to forty-two. This was due perhaps to the fact that Liberal voters, who in 1923 had seen their votes lead to a Labour Government, now voted Conservative 'to play safe'. It is difficult to see, therefore, that the 'Zinoviev Letter' could have had a profound effect on the fortunes of the Labour Party in the 1924 election, and indeed, as Professor Lyman suggests, it 'did no more than sharpen the outlines of the election results' (**67**, p. 269).

Despite the short time it lasted the Labour Government of 1924 remains of major importance in the history of the Labour Party. Most commentators agree that during their nine months of office the Labour Ministers performed 'creditably', and proved to their party and to the country that they could govern. But it was 'good government' by conventional standards only. What Labour had not done was to introduce socialism, or produce any great breakthrough in a major aspect of national policy. It failed (as we have seen) to come to grips with the greatest domestic problem of the interwar period — unemployment; and even MacDonald's successes in the field did little to settle definitely the continuous tug-of-war between 'realists' and 'utopians' within the party over problems of foreign policy, a situation that was to last until the very eve of the Second World War. Nor did the party do very much to learn from its mistakes during the next five years of opposition. Because it was a minority government in 1924 it could prove to its own satisfaction that all that could have been done had been done, while the 'Zinoviev Letter' provided the perfect alibi for its defeat at the general election of that year. This was not true of the I.L.P. leaders, but, despite their growing disillusionment with their former idol, there was no real challenge to MacDonald's leadership after 1924, nor, even more remarkably, to Snowden's record at the Treasury (**100**).

Professor Trevor Wilson has suggested that the responsibility for the downfall of the first Labour Government lies with Labour itself. 'Requiring active Liberal support to retain office', he writes, 'Labour responded not by conciliating or even ignoring the Liberals, but by seeking to pulverise them' (**31**, p. 289). But Labour believed that the bulk of the Liberal Party had no genuine sympathy with their programme, and, with Lloyd George back in the fold, could not really be trusted. 'There are only two Parties in Politics today', said MacDonald in the Commons in 1923. 'There is the Capitalist Party and the Labour and Socialist Party'. More important, they had convinced themselves ever since 1918 that, in the long run, the way to real power for their party lay through the destruction of the Liberal Party as a potential alternative government. Whatever their other sins of omission, that at least they achieved in 1924, even though, as Wilson suggests, the long run was to be very long indeed.

4 Labour's Time of Trial

THE GENERAL STRIKE AND THE SECOND LABOUR GOVERNMENT

The most important event in the years immediately following the end of the first Labour Government was the General Strike of 1926, and many commentators have seen this dispute as evidence of a more militant mood among the leaders of the industrial (though not the political) arm of the Labour Movement. There is something in this. Yet during these years the moderates within the Trades Union Congress, led by Ernest Bevin and Walter Citrine, still retained firm control; and it would be wrong to see the General Strike itself as indicating, either in its origins or its ideas, a new departure in the history of British trade unionism. Rather, the General Strike was the outcome of yet another round in the bitter and obstinate struggle between men and owners that had typified the coal industry since at least the end of the First World War. Once again, in 1925, the mineowners aimed at solving the deep-rooted problems of their industry by imposing wage cuts and longer hours on their labour force. Once again, the miners responded in the famous slogan of their militant leader, A. J. Cook, 'Not a minute on the day, not a penny off the pay!' In their defiance the miners were now backed by the great unions in the T.U.C., eager perhaps to eradicate the shame of their previous betrayal on 'Black Friday' in 1921, and seeing in the miners the frontline troops in the defence of working-class living standards against a new capitalist offensive. At first, under the threat of this new trade union unity the Conservative Government backed down, on 31 July 1925 ('*Red* Friday'), and agreed to continue its subsidy to the coal industry until a new Royal Commission, headed by Sir Herbert Samuel, had once again investigated its state of health and proposed remedies. The Samuel Commission reported in March 1926. It recommended long-term reforms for the industry, accompanied however by immediate wage reductions, which the miners' leaders once again rejected. The Government therefore abandoned its attempt to impose a settlement on the owners, and prepared to face a showdown with the T.U.C. leaders over their support for a general strike in support of the miners, which none of them really wanted but to which they were now committed. On 1 May 1926 the miners' strike began; and on the same day the Government declared a national emergency and began to put into action its carefully laid plans to combat a general strike which it had quietly prepared during the previous nine months' respite. Negotiations broke down between the T.U.C. leaders and the Government on the night of 2-3 May. On the following morning the General Strike began.

The General Strike was a unique and extraordinary phenomenon in British history (**110**). From one point of view it can be seen as a noble and unselfish attempt by the working class to use their industrial power in defence of the miners' standard of life. From another point of view it was the last and greatest attempt by the British trade union movement to put to the test the old syndicalist doctrine of 'direct action', and thus obtain their industrial demands by holding the community up to ransom. The leaders of the T.U.C., however, did not see the revolutionary implications of the weapon they were using, and it broke in their hands. For though the strike was remarkably successful in terms of the solidarity and loyalty of the workers, it was not decisive as far as its ultimate purpose was concerned, namely to force the Government to reopen negotiations. When it became clear after the first few days that the Government would not yield to their pressure, Ernest Bevin and his colleagues were faced with the alternatives either of continuing and widening the strike — which in their eyes would have appalling consequences — or abandoning what had now become a pointless struggle. Sir Herbert Samuel's proposed mediation gave them a way of escape; and, though the rank-and-file were still solid in support and the miners were hotly opposed to their 'betrayal', the strike was called off by the T.U.C. on the morning of 12 May. In effect it was an unconditional surrender. The miners carried on alone for another six months until through sheer exhaustion they returned to work on worse terms than they had been offered earlier.

The failure of the General Strike represents a profound turning point in the history of British trade unionism. Indirectly, it laid the ghost of that philosophy of 'direct action' which had fascinated the trade union world for so long, and which had now been tried and found wanting. 'It was', as Beatrice Webb said, 'a proletarian distemper which had to run its course' (**116**, p. 65). Nineteen twenty-six was followed by a considerable decline in strikes; and, as exemplified by the Mond-Turner Talks in 1927 (in which Ernest Bevin was really the T.U.C.'s spokesman) an attempt by some union leaders to work with the employers in settling common industrial problems. But for the Labour Movement as a whole the General Strike of 1926 did have one bitter aftermath: the

Trade Union Act of 1927. This outlawed not only the 'general' and 'sympathetic' strike, but, in an act of vindictive political spite by right-wing Conservatives, replaced the principle of 'contracting out' (as embodied in the 1913 Trade Union Act) by 'contracting in', in the hope that the apathy of trade unionists would lead to a slump in their affiliations to the Labour Party. In this presumption the Conservatives were fully justified. The number of trade union members affiliated to the Labour Party fell by more than a million by the end of 1928; and indeed over the longer period from 1928 to 1945 (the last year before the Act was repealed) the proportion of trade unionists subscribing to their union's political fund fell by about a third (91).

Thus from the point of view of trade union affiliations and finance the Labour Party lost heavily as a result of the General Strike. On the other hand, in a number of less tangible ways, it probably gained. For the cost and failure of industrial action confirmed the faith of the Labour Movement's leaders in political action; and, as after Taff Vale, resentment at the 1927 Act tended to increase trade union support for the Labour Party, which in any case was now forced to concentrate more on building up its individual membership — a healthy development. All this strengthened the position of Ramsay MacDonald [doc. 23]. He had played no part in the General Strike at all, having been warned off by Ernest Bevin. In private, however, the Labour Leader was critical of the trade unions' tactics, and shortly after the strike was over he wrote in the *Socialist Review*:

> The General Strike is a weapon that cannot be wielded for industrial purposes. It is clumsy and ineffectual. . . . I hope that the result will be a thorough reconsideration of trade union tactics. If the wonderful unity in the strike . . . would be shown in politics, Labour could solve the mining and similar difficulties through the ballot box (113, i, 349).

It cannot be said, however, that between the first and second Labour Governments the party's attitude towards the country's problems justified this rather facile optimism. The Independent Labour Party, under the leadership of James Maxton, was now increasingly hostile to MacDonald's 'reformism'; and in 1925 it had produced its own programme, *Socialism in Our Time*, which, though it supported a 'planned economy', was by no means an extremist document. It was, nevertheless, too much for MacDonald and Snowden; and in 1927, as a result of the I.L.P.'s attempt to compete with the Labour Party in ideas and organisation, they severed their long connection with that body. The Labour Party then produced its own statement of long-term objectives in *Labour and the Nation* (1928), which added little to Webb's programme of ten years earlier. The party's election manifesto, produced the following year, failed to mention socialism at all and concentrated on the unemployment problem, but the measures suggested lacked either 'bite' or conviction. In cogency and originality the Labour Party's thinking on social and economic problems was in fact far behind that of the Liberal Party, which, under the leadership of Lloyd George (Asquith died in 1928) produced in the same year the famous *Yellow Book* on Britain's industrial future, strongly marked by Keynesian ideas, and a dynamic electoral programme, *We Can Conquer Unemployment*, shortly afterwards. The Conservative Government meanwhile coasted along quietly under its banner of 'Safety First!' until its five-year term expired in 1929 and, for no especial reason, a general election took place.

In a sense, therefore, as Skidelsky has argued of this period, the real cleavage was not between socialists and capitalists, but between 'economic radicals' and 'economic conservatives', and this cut across party lines (77). But this profound economic debate failed to stir the minds of an electorate now increased by the 'flapper vote', and the campaign itself was dull and undramatic. The Liberals did badly, despite the attractiveness of their programme, and the fact that, like the other two parties, they put up over five hundred candidates; they polled over five million votes but gained only fifty-nine seats. The Labour and Conservative polls were both close — over eight million votes each — giving the Conservatives 260 and Labour 288 seats. Labour was therefore for the first time the largest party in the House of Commons, and it appeared that MacDonald's constitutional and moderate policies had paid off. Once again, however, his party lacked an overall majority. Nevertheless, since the electorate had clearly voted against the Conservative Party, Baldwin resigned on 4 June 1929 and Ramsay MacDonald became Prime Minister for the second time.

MacDonald's second Cabinet was not markedly different from the first: with Snowden once again at the Treasury, it was clearly right-wing in outlook, and the only prominent left-winger represented was George Lansbury, who was tucked away at the Ministry of Works. There was some reshuffling of posts among the inner hierarchy of ex-ministers, and MacDonald at last yielded the Foreign Office to Henderson. But though a number of outstanding young men like Hugh Dalton and Oswald Mosley were given junior posts, the tone of the Government was set by the small group of senior ministers, led by MacDonald and Snowden, now ageing rapidly and set in their ideas. The Government was in a slightly stronger position than in 1924 since Labour this time was the largest group in the House, and the Liberal Party were prepared to support radical measures. In this expectation, however, they were sadly disillusioned. In foreign affairs, it is true, the Government had a fair record of achievement. Arthur Henderson carried through his policies of conciliation, arbitration and cooperation through the League of Nations with considerable short-term success, despite obstruction by both MacDonald, and Snowden in his role as an economic John Bull (57). This cleared the way for Henderson's outstanding support for disarmament which soon earned him the Presidency of the World Disarmament Conference. This policy was given some practical support by the conclusion in 1930 of an agreement in favour of naval limitation by Great Britain, Japan and the United States. Diplomatic relations were again restored with the Soviet Union, and ambassadors were exchanged for the first time; but in the absence of real goodwill on both sides little else was achieved. Nor was the Government very successful in conciliating the rising nationalist temper in India, or those countries in the Middle East for which Great Britain was responsible.

In domestic affairs the Government's record was uninspiring. A few minor social reforms were passed; useful 'rationalisation' schemes were introduced for the coal and agricultural industries; and Herbert Morrison, as Minister of Transport, put forward his great scheme for the establishment of the London Passenger Transport Board, which was implemented by his successor in 1933. But the MacDonald Government got little credit, either then or later, for any of these policies, since its achievements in both domestic and foreign affairs were overshadowed by its gigantic failure over unemployment. It was their failure after 1929 to reduce the steadily increasing numbers of unemployed that sapped the will and confidence of the Labour Ministers and left them in a desperately weak position to grapple with the even greater problems that faced them in the crises of 1931.

1931: ECONOMIC AND POLITICAL CRISIS

Large-scale unemployment had been a feature of the British economy since the beginning of the postwar slump; and, as we have seen, it had been one of the main problems that had taxed the first Labour Government. When MacDonald assumed office for the second time in 1929 unemployment was already over a million; a year later, partly as a result of the Great Crash in the United States which disrupted trade and led to the withdrawal of American funds from Europe, it was more than two million. This great army of the workless, mainly in the old mining and manufacturing areas of the country, existed on the 'dole'; that is, payments of one sort or another from the Unemployment Insurance Fund, whose mounting expenditure horrified and alarmed orthodox business and financial opinion. For socialists, like George Orwell, for example, the existence of mass unemployment bore eloquent testimony to the failures of the capitalist system (24).

J. H. Thomas, the ebullient cockney ex-railwayman, was given responsibility for unemployment policy by MacDonald, helped by a small committee which included Lansbury and Oswald Mosley, then Chancellor of the Duchy of Lancaster. It soon became clear that Thomas had neither the stature nor the intellectual grasp to cope with the immensity of his task; and his suggested expedients — large-scale road development, for example — were in any case hindered by Snowden's rigidity at the Treasury. Oswald Mosley was the only member of the Committee who knew exactly what he wanted; and his bold and imaginative plans for an expansionist economic policy have made him the one heroic figure in the dismal story of the 'Politicians and the Slump'. Mosley's Memorandum of February 1930, in which he described his ideas in detail, was rejected, really on grounds of expense, by the Cabinet, and therefore inevitably by the Parliamentary Party. Despite a brilliant speech by Mosley in its defence it was also defeated, though narrowly, by the Party Conference in October — still loyal to MacDonald and Snowden and suspicious of this aristocratic and arrogant outsider. In disgust, instead of fighting for his ideas, Mosley resigned from the Labour Party, founded a 'New Party', and eventually, as is well known, ended up as the Führer of the British Union of Fascists, thus damning himself in the eyes of all respectable opinion (129). MacDonald was sensible enough, however, to remove Thomas from his uncongenial post, and he himself assumed personal responsibility for unemployment policy.

In 1930 the economic position grew worse as the effects of the worldwide depression were reflected in declining production and trade in Great Britain, a collapse of foreign investment, increasing unemployment, and a growing burden on the Treasury. MacDonald was in a difficult position. A tyro himself in economics, he was forced to rely for economic advice on others. On the one hand there was the Treasury, and Snowden with his burning devotion to 'Economy, Free Trade and Gold'; on the other, the businessmen, trade unionists and professional economists (including, notably, Keynes and Pigou) as represented on that proto-'Brains-Trust', the Economic Advisory Council, set up at the beginning of 1930. Unfortunately, since the businessmen on the council could never agree with the economists, and the economists found it difficult to agree completely among themselves, the Prime Minister was never given that firm practical advice with which he could combat the grim orthodoxies of Snowden and the Treasury. Given the contradictory advice he received, the increasing attacks of the opposition parties on the wastefulness of Government expenditure, and his party's anomalous parliamentary position, it was inevitable that MacDonald should seek to obtain general party agreement for his handling of the country's economic problems. The eventual outcome of this approach was the establishment in March 1931 of the May Committee (chaired by Sir George May, Secretary of the Prudential Assurance Company), on which all three parties were represented, to investigate the country's financial position. It was at this point that events in central Europe impinged on the weakened financial position of this country, to convert a domestic into a financial crisis. For the collapse of the Austrian Credit Anstalt in May 1931 was followed by bank collapses in Germany; and when the German government proceeded to freeze all its foreign assets on 15 July, the strain was transferred to London and other western European financial centres. London, with its overvalued currency (the result of the return to gold in 1925), its relatively small gold reserves, and £90 million of assets locked up in Germany, started to lose gold at the rate of £4 million a day. On 28 July, however, loans of £25 million each were obtained in New York and Paris, and it is possible that a return to stability might have been achieved. What shattered this prospect was the publication on 31 July of the May Report. 'The appearance of such a document at this particular time', writes Skidelsky, 'converted what had in essence been a technical financial crisis into a crisis of confidence in the Government and the country' (78).

The May Report concluded that there would be a Budget deficiency of £120 million in 1932. The only way for the Government to avoid financial disaster was by a policy of rigorous retrenchment. It proposed, therefore, governmental economies to the tune of £97 million, including £67 million lopped off unemployment benefit; the rest of the deficit would be overcome by increased taxation. As most commentators now agree, the May Committee's diagnosis was faulty and many of its proposals were bound to worsen the country's financial position; indeed the two Labour members on the Committee produced a Minority Report which was much more sensible in its proposals. But in that pre-Keynesian age, when belief in the gold standard and a balanced Budget were regarded as fundamental articles of faith (though even Keynes believed at the time that the gold standard *should* be defended), the May Report, with its firm affirmation of economic truth, seemed to show the way to financial salvation. MacDonald and Snowden therefore accepted almost unquestioningly its major principles; but with incredible ineptitude they departed for the summer vacation without giving any public hint of their attitude towards the Report, thus allowing it to breed gloom and mistrust.

The Prime Minister and the Chancellor were in fact astonishingly slow to see its implications, not only for the immediate financial position of the country, but for the future of the Labour Government itself. The despondency produced by the May Report increased the drain on sterling; and, following the bankers' warnings, MacDonald returned to London from his Scottish retreat on 11 August. It was now taken for granted by the Treasury and the Bank of England that in order to restore confidence in the pound, the budget must be balanced: a vigorous programme of cuts, on the lines recommended by the May Committee, was absolutely necessary. The Prime Minister agreed. 'We are of one mind', he said on arriving back in London, ' – we intend to balance the budget'. MacDonald's immediate political task, therefore, was to find a programme of cuts which would be acceptable to his cabinet colleagues (with the T.U.C. leaders lowering grimly in the background) and also to the Opposition parties, since only with the latter's support could the proposals be carried through Parliament. This was a task of extreme difficulty which in the end MacDonald, at least as head of a Labour Cabinet, found it impossible to fulfil.

On 12 August the five members of the Cabinet Economy Committee (MacDonald, Snowden, Henderson, Thomas and Graham) got to work. They agreed fairly easily on cuts in the pay of teachers, police etc. which amounted to more than £30 million, and to a ten per cent cut in unemployment insurance payments amounting to £38 million – the May Committee had proposed a twenty per cent cut of £67 million! But they refused to cut the standard rate of unemployment benefit and this became the nub of the whole dispute during the next twelve days. The final economy figure agreed on by the Committee, to be laid before the full Cabinet, was £78 million. The Cabinet, however, which met on Wednesday, 19 August, went back on some of the proposed changes in unemployment benefit suggested by the Economy Committee and agreed, provisionally, on cuts of only £56 million, and for the moment MacDonald and Snowden had to be content with this figure. On the following morning the two men saw the Opposition leaders, who rejected the proposed cuts as inadequate; in the evening they and the other members of the Economy Committee saw the T.U.C. leaders, headed by Bevin and Citrine, who, since they completely opposed the May Committee's diagnosis, rejected the whole programme of cuts, and suggested import duties, heavier taxation and suspension of the Sinking Fund (**113**, i). 'The General Council are pigs', commented Sidney Webb to his wife. At the Cabinet meeting on the following day, Friday 21 August, the majority of the members, led by Arthur Henderson (who had been very impressed by the T.U.C.'s arguments), refused to budge beyond the figure of £56 million, and this became the final figure that MacDonald, reluctantly, agreed to place once more before the Opposition leaders.

Financial events now outstripped the deliberations of the politicians and delivered them into the hands of the bankers. That same evening, Sir Ernest Harvey, the Deputy Governor of the Bank of England, told MacDonald that the Government's dilatoriness in finalising the economy plans had accelerated the flight from the pound: immediate credits were now urgently needed from New York and Paris, and these, he intimated, would only be forthcoming if the Government adopted a 'tough' policy of cuts, particularly in unemployment expenditure. Once more, on the following Saturday morning, MacDonald met his Cabinet: the only concession they would agree on, however, was that the Prime Minister (without committing the Cabinet) might test the attitude of the Opposition leaders and the New York bankers to the suggestion that a further £20 million be added to the list of economies by a ten per cent cut in the standard rate of unemployment benefit. By the afternoon the Opposition leaders had approved. Everything now depended on the message from New York. Late that evening, while the Cabinet waited impatiently in the garden at Number 10, Downing Street, a message arrived from Harrison, the Governor of the New York Federal Reserve Bank. It approved a fresh loan, but only after Parliament had ratified an economy programme that, in the Governor's words, had 'the sincere approval and support of the Bank of England and the City generally' (**78**). Since MacDonald believed that these conditions were already fulfilled, the only thing wanting now was the approval of the Labour Cabinet to the ten per cent cut. When the Cabinet reassembled, the Prime Minister made a final eloquent plea for acceptance. The proposals as a whole represented, he said, 'the negation of everything that the Labour Party stood for, yet he was absolutely satisfied that it was necessary in the national interest to implement them if the country was to be secured' (**78**). In the end it appeared that eleven ministers, including MacDonald, voted for the ten per cent cut, and nine opposed. Since the minority included such leading ministers as Henderson, Clynes and Graham, the resignation of the second Labour Government became inevitable.

Shortly after ten o'clock MacDonald left for the Palace with the collective resignation of the Cabinet in his pocket, and most of his colleagues probably expected shortly the formation of a Conservative/ Liberal Ministry. But early that morning, unbeknown to them, MacDonald had seen the King and told him that, owing to disagreements, it was likely that his Government would break up; it was essential, therefore, that a new government be installed immediately that happened. The King thereupon saw the two Opposition leaders, Sir Herbert Samuel (Lloyd George was ill) and Stanley Baldwin, and at the former's suggestion proposed the formation of a National Government under Ramsay MacDonald if the Labour Government did collapse. Baldwin agreed 'for the sake of the country', though for both Liberals and Conservatives there were obvious party advantages to be gained from MacDonald continuing as Prime Minister if a drastic economy programme was to be implemented. At ten o'clock on Monday morning, 24 August 1931, MacDonald saw the King; and at noon he announced to his bemused colleagues at the last meeting of the Labour Cabinet that he had agreed to head a National Government for the purpose of meeting the present emergency only, and asked for their support. Only three members agreed to follow him — Thomas, Sankey and Snowden — and shortly afterwards the members dispersed. Thus by a strange metamorphosis Ramsay MacDonald, who had been appointed head of a Labour Government in 1929, ended up two years later as the leader of a National Government in which the Labour Ministers were a minority [doc. 24].

How are we to explain MacDonald's conduct? It is probably true that, as his critics aver, he was vain, ambitious, and increasingly out of touch with rank-and-file sentiment within the party, and this helps to explain his inability to appreciate the depth of feeling over the ten per cent cut. But there is no real evidence, as Bassett has shown, that MacDonald was either in sympathy with or had been planning to become leader of a 'National Government' before the events of August 1931 thrust that role upon him. For a generation after this crisis Ramsay MacDonald was branded as a traitor to the Labour movement; but most impartial historians now agree with the spirit of Bassett's remark that 'he was moved primarily by his sense of duty', even though we need not accept his further implication that what was good for MacDonald was also good for the Labour Party (52). What gave weight to MacDonald's actions too was his belief that his leadership of a National Government would be temporary: as he stressed to his colleagues at that last fateful Cabinet meeting, it was to deal with an extraordinary crisis only, and, as had happened after 1918, he would return to the fold later on to lead a reunited Party. For his Labour colleagues, as MacDonald himself seems to have accepted, the position was different: for them the primary issue was one of party loyalty and not the question of the unemployment cuts (over which the gap between the two groups was very narrow), or a vague 'national interest' over whose meaning no one could agree. After all, a majority of the Cabinet had supported all the cuts, and even the minority must have expected that they would in any case be imposed by the next Conservative/Liberal Government. For most Labour Ministers the major question was, therefore, as Professor Medlicott has emphasised, how to avoid a major split within the party, and on this issue a majority preferred to resign together rather than follow the Prime Minister into the National Government and accept a major breach in the Cabinet and the party (22, p. 261).

This analysis of motives, though fascinating to the psychologist, is now relatively unimportant to the historian: the real question to be asked about MacDonald's behaviour in August 1931, Skidelsky suggests, is how 'under his leadership the Labour Government had drifted into a position which left it so little choice' (77, p. 426). The answer to this question, he believes, lies in the economic failures of the Labour Government *before* the crisis in the summer of 1931; and their failures were a necessary consequence of the 'Utopian ethic' to which the party was committed.

> The Labour Party's commitment to a nebulous Socialism [Skidelsky writes] made it regard the work of the 'economic radicals' such as Keynes as mere 'tinkering', when in fact it was they who were providing the real choice. It was the failure of the Labour Party to recognise that this was the choice that doomed it to failure and sterility in this crucial period (77, p. 12).

In a recent article Skidelsky has gone further, and argued that the Labour Party's failure was a failure not so much of socialism itself, but of Victorian liberalism, the parent ideology from which British socialism sprang and which, in its economic aspect at least, had persisted virtually unchallenged well into the twentieth century (79). Skidelsky's main thesis, and its later refinement, both seem to exaggerate the influence of ideas, or their absence, as an explanation of economic and political events. When we reflect on the economic problems that faced another Labour Prime Minister, Harold Wilson, in the 1960s, even though (unlike MacDonald) he possessed both a parliamentary majority, the 'best' possible economic advice, and no particular commitment to a 'Utopian ethic', it may perhaps be suggested that the second Labour Government's economic failures have rather deeper roots than Skidelsky suggests.

On 25 August MacDonald announced his new Cabinet of Ten, consisting of four Conservatives, two Liberals and three Labour men — Sankey, Thomas and Snowden: about a dozen other Labour backbenchers supported him. He had hoped for more Labour support; but on that same day the T.U.C. in effect took over the Parliamentary Labour Party and disowned MacDonald's leadership. A few weeks later he was formally expelled from the party. The National Government had, however, been formed to balance the budget and introduce economies, and this Snowden proceeded to do in his Budget on 8 September. Virtue had its reward when the hoped-for loans were received from Paris and New York; but this did little to restore confidence — a situation which was worsened by the Invergordon Mutiny of the Atlantic Fleet on 15 September — and the drain on gold continued. On 21 September 1931, therefore, Britain abandoned the gold standard. Bank rate was then raised to six per cent, and for the moment this brought to an end the long-drawn-out financial crisis. As Taylor comments: 'A few days before, a managed currency had seemed as wicked as family planning. Now, like contraception, it became a commonplace. This was the end of an age' (**30**, p. 297).

So it was too for the Labour Party. Following these dramatic events MacDonald saw the need for a general election to restore unity and confidence, and in October 1931 he appealed to the country for a 'doctor's mandate' to deal with the economic crisis. The result was a landslide for the National Government: it won 556 seats and gained more than seventy per cent of the popular vote. What probably gave MacDonald and his supporters their extraordinary victory was the association in the minds of the electorate between the Labour Party and the depression, and the conviction that only a national government could grapple effectively with the problems facing the country.

MacDonald's personal position was tragic: rejected by his old party, his own National Labour group numbered thirteen members, and, with 471 Conservatives in the House he was, like the National Liberals also, their prisoner. For the Labour Party the election was a disaster. It lost two million votes compared with 1929, and now numbered only forty-six members, little more than its prewar total. Of the older leaders, only Lansbury was returned, and he became Leader of the Parliamentary Party. Thus, as in 1918, the power and prestige of the parliamentary wing of the party slumped, and control passed more and more into the capable hands of Bevin, Citrine and the T.U.C. The MacDonald era was over.

5 Revival and Triumph

LABOUR IN THE 1930s

The 1930s were in many ways an unhappy period for the Labour Party. Condemned to permanent opposition, suffering still from the traumatic shock administered by the events of 1931, and faced increasingly with difficult and distasteful problems in foreign affairs, the party became more inward-looking, monolithic and conformist, though on the other hand it also endeavoured to become more realistic in its attitude towards domestic problems. Thus the increasing influence of the trade unions within the inner circle of the Party was made more explicit by altering the constitution of the old National Joint Council, on which the T.U.C., the Labour Party Executive and the Parliamentary Labour Party had had equal representation, and giving the T.U.C. half the representation on a new body, the National Council of Labour. It was this council (where the influence of Bevin was so important) that came to concern itself primarily with the Labour Party's policy decisions; it was the National Executive that became particularly preoccupied with the details of party programmes and plans for projected legislation. Here its approach was much more specific and detailed than during the MacDonald era. In this field the Executive's work was done mainly through its Policy Sub-Committee, where men like Dalton and Morrison were especially prominent; and the plans they produced on topics such as banking, land, transport etc., became, during this decade, the basis for Labour's published programmes – *For Socialism and Peace*, 1934; and *Labour's Immediate Programme*, 1937 – and subsequently of much of the legislation of the 1945 Labour Government.

Despite the break with MacDonald in 1931 the Independent Labour Party persisted in its hostility to the 'reformism' of the Labour Party leadership, and disaffiliated from the party in the following year; a decision which was followed by the I.L.P.'s long and painful decline. Moreover, the Labour Party still set its face firmly against the Communist Party, and indeed took stronger measures to prevent infiltration into the party by, or association of party members with, Communist 'front' organisations. The Labour Party 'is entitled', as Morrison said, 'to take exceptional measures to protect itself from their activity' (**56**,

p. 165). Left-wing feeling, however, partly as a reaction against the 'betrayal' of 1931 and all that it implied, was still strong among sections of the party; and now it was given a more directly intellectual expression by the writings of publicists like Harold Laski and John Strachey and, more important, the political leadership of Sir Stafford Cripps, the rising hope of the stern unbending militants. This attitude was seen not only in the leftish tone of the 1932 Party Conference, for example, but also in the rise of the left-wing Socialist League which, though it began as a research and propaganda group within the Labour Movement, became, like the old I.L.P., more and more a 'party within a party', and thus incurred the deeprooted suspicion of the Labour Establishment.

Labour's predilection for 'playing safe' in the years immediately following the disaster of 1931 was seen in the appointment of party officials, and particularly in the choice of a party leader. In 1932 George Lansbury became nominal leader of the party, since he was the only senior member returned to the House of Commons in the previous election; and Clement Attlee, also one of the few survivors, became his deputy. When Lansbury retired as leader after the 1935 Party Conference, mainly as a result of the disputes over foreign policy described below, he was succeeded, provisionally, by Attlee, whose task was to carry the party through the forthcoming general election. After the election Attlee stood against Morrison and Greenwood, both now in the House of Commons, and was confirmed as party leader, mainly because of the strong support he received from the rank-and-file in the Parliamentary Party who saw in him a man who could be 'trusted', someone in fact who was in every way the exact antithesis of Ramsay MacDonald. Even so, the Party constitution was changed so as to make it more difficult for the party leader to assume office without the consent of the Party Executive.

In a steady unspectacular way, therefore, with new leaders, rising individual membership and definite programmes, Labour began to win back some of the ground lost in 1931, a task in which it was helped also by the National Government's resignation in the face of mass unemployment at home and an increasingly strident nationalism abroad. Labour gained control of the London County Council in 1934 and won ten by-elections between 1931 and 1935, including the famous East Fulham seat, regarded as a victory for Labour's policy of 'collective security'.

The success of this steady advance was seen in the general election of 1935, fought on behalf of the National Government by Stanley Baldwin, since MacDonald had been quietly pushed out of the premiership by the Conservative Party earlier that year. Labour won 154 seats (a gain of more than a hundred since 1931) which meant the return of most of the leading members of the party: but the National Government, with 431 seats, still retained an enormous majority. In terms of popular votes, however, the verdict was reasonably close: eleven-and-a-half million votes for the Government, and about ten million votes against. Labour's share of the poll remained fairly steady (at just over thirty-seven per cent it was slightly better than in 1929, and even in 1931 it did not fall below thirty per cent), and Baldwin won because his Government was still able to command the allegiance of most Liberal voters, as seen in the slump, for example, in the number of Independent Liberals returned. Perhaps more than for any other election of the interwar period, the 1935 election turned on issues of foreign policy. The Labour Party supported collective security through the League of Nations, without being really agreed on what that meant; but so now did the Government — 'a death-bed repentance' in Attlee's phrase.

It was indeed questions of foreign policy that dominated discussions within the Labour Party during the troubled years between the rise of Hitler and the outbreak of the Second World War. In the early 'thirties the Labour Party still clung to its policy of peace and disarmament, as indicated by the resolutions passed by the 1934 Party Conference. The National Council, however, produced its own policy statements, urging a more realistic assessment of the international situation, and the famous 'Peace Ballot' of 1935 showed that many people were prepared to support military sanctions against an aggressor. The events of that year, in fact, indicated all too clearly the ambiguities and confusions in Labour foreign policy. On the one hand, the Parliamentary Party voted against the Government's air estimates, causing Dalton to observe gloomily: 'The party won't face up to realities. There is still much mere anti-armament sentiment, and many are more agin' our own Government than agin' Hitler. Pretty desperate' (**119**, p. 88). On the other hand, the General Council and the Party Executive were strongly in favour of real sanctions against Italy, following her invasion of Abyssinia in October 1935, even if it implied war. The Labour Party Conference which met in the same month therefore provided an opportunity for a showdown between the protagonists of the different points of view. Both Cripps and Lansbury, the nominal leader of the party, opposed the Executive's resolutions: Cripps, on 'socialist' grounds, Lansbury, because of his pacifist convictions. Both men were brutally lambasted by Ernest Bevin in one of his most famous broadsides, and on the whole he won the day [**doc. 25**]. Cripps could take it; Lansbury, now an old man and assured of the affection and respect of the party, retired as leader, and was shortly afterwards succeeded by Attlee.

The events on the international scene in 1935-36 — Abyssinia, the German reoccupation of the Rhineland, the beginning of the Spanish Civil War — seemed to give countenance to the views of both the Left and the Right within the party. Bevin and Dalton could argue that British rearmament was now vital, particularly in view of the League's failures. Cripps could insist, on the other hand, that rearmament must still be opposed since the National Government's attitude to these events showed that it was both hypocritical and untrustworthy. This januslike attitude was seen at the Edinburgh Conference of the party in 1936, when a compromise resolution was passed which supported collective security but opposed rearmament. Nevertheless, the helplessness of the League and the feebleness of the National Government in the face of aggression abroad, did encourage sympathy for the left-wing point of view. This led to the demand by Cripps and his supporters for a 'Popular Front' of all left-wing parties — the Socialist League, the I.L.P., and the Communists — to combat both Fascism and the National Government; views which were both expressed and symbolised by the Left Book Club, founded by the publisher, Victor Gollancz, in 1936 (**96**). The Labour Executive, however, refused to have anything to do with the idea of associating with Communists, 'to achieve', as they said, 'a spurious unity with those who hold principles so completely irreconcilable with Labour' (**56**, p. 191); and in the end the intransigence of Cripps and his supporters over this issue led to their expulsion from the party in the spring of 1939, and the disaffiliation of the Socialist League. The only concession made to leftist sentiment was to alter the party's constitution so as to allow the constituency parties to elect separately their own delegates to the National Executive, and these were increased from five to seven. As a result, intellectuals like Professor Laski and D. N. Pritt gained places on the Executive, where they were still entrapped by the dominant trade union majority.

By that time, in fact, despite the vociferousness of the Left, the tide had turned in favour of the right-wingers within the party. In 1936 Dalton became Chairman of the National Executive, and Ernest Bevin Chairman of the General Council of the T.U.C., and they were thus able to use their influence more directly in favour of their policies. In 1937 Dalton got the Parliamentary Party to support the forces' estimates; and in the same year the Bournemouth Party Conference at last definitely supported rearmament, even though the Left still argued, in the words of Aneurin Bevan, that such a policy would 'put a sword in the hands of our enemies that may be used to cut off our own heads'. From the point of view of Labour foreign policy, that conference marked (in Naylor's phrase) 'a decisive turning point'. 'After Bournemouth', he writes, '... Labour advocated a firm and honourable international policy, buttressed at last by a commitment to rearmament' (73, p. 207). This new firmness was seen in the Labour Party's strong opposition towards Neville Chamberlain's policy of appeasing Nazi Germany in the course of the next two years – years which witnessed the annexation of Austria, the destruction of the Czechoslovak state, and the German invasion of Poland. Finally, the party firmly supported the British declaration of war on Germany on 3 September 1939; though, inconsistent to the last, they had a few months earlier voted against conscription. Once the war began, the internal squabbles within the party became trivial and irrelevant. Compared with 1914, the Labour Party entered the Second World War united and resolute in its determination to defeat Nazism, and to create a better postwar world.

THE SECOND WORLD WAR AND THE 1945 GENERAL ELECTION

Once war was declared an 'electoral truce' was agreed on by the three major political parties. Since Labour, however, owing to its bitter distrust of Chamberlain, was not prepared to join the Government, the Prime Minister was forced to strengthen his team by the inclusion of a number of dissident Tories, notably Winston Churchill, who became once again First Lord of the Admiralty, and Eden. During the period of the 'phony war' the Labour Party acted in the House of Commons as critical supporters of Chamberlain's Government, pressing for a more effective mobilisation of the nation's resources. The uneasiness which they, and many Conservative members, felt at the tepid war leadership of Neville Chamberlain came to a head in the spring of 1940, when, following the German attack on Scandinavia, the British forces in Norway, after a badly handled campaign, were forced to withdraw ignominiously. In the debate that followed – marked by Leopold Amery's Cromwellian outburst against the Prime Minister, 'In the name of God, go' – Chamberlain's majority slumped to eighty-one, and it was clear that he had lost the confidence of an important section of his party. He still believed, however, that his premiership might be saved if he could obtain the support of the Labour Party. On 9 May, therefore, he invited Attlee and Greenwood to see him, in the presence of Churchill and Halifax, his putative successors, to discuss the conditions on which they might agree to prop up his Government. Attlee refused to commit himself without consulting his party, then in conference at Bournemouth; but Churchill, who kept his counsel throughout, sensed that his moment had come. On the following day, marked by the commencement of the German onslaught against the Low Countries, Attlee telephoned the Prime Minister from Bournemouth to inform him that the Labour Party would be prepared to join a new Government, but not under *his* leadership. Thereupon Chamberlain resigned. Later that evening Winston Churchill agreed to form a new Government and, in consultation with Attlee, the major posts were distributed.

Partly as a reward for the role it had played in the formation of the new Government, partly as a recognition of its real strength in the country, Labour did well out of the allocation of offices. Attlee and Greenwood became members of the small War Cabinet of five; Ernest Bevin was given the key post of Minister of Labour and later entered the War Cabinet; Morrison, Alexander and Dalton were given important positions, and Jowitt became Solicitor-General. There was some re-shuffling of offices later on; Morrison, for example, was soon moved to the more congenial post of Home Secretary and Dalton to the Board of Trade, and new men, including Stafford Cripps (now restored to re-spectability), were brought in; but the same rough balance was main-tained between the parties. On the whole the new Coalition Govern-ment worked more smoothly than its predecessor had done during the First World War, and the part played in it by the Labour Ministers was outstanding and indispensable. Their contribution was mainly on the Home Front. 'Grand strategy' was left to the Prime Minister. Ernest Bevin dealt with the major task of directing and organising the British labour force in a tough but conciliatory spirit; Herbert Morrison proved to be a capable and popular Home Secretary; while the contribution of other ministers, such as Dalton, was sound and effective. In many ways, however, it was Attlee's success as a minister, though untrumpeted at the time, that was the most remarkable. As Deputy Prime Minister he presided over the Cabinet during Churchill's frequent forays abroad in a sensible and businesslike way, and in effect supervised home affairs throughout these war years (141). As a result, his stature with his Cabinet colleagues, and especially with Ernest Bevin, increased enor-mously, and the remarkable trust and admiration that developed between the two widely contrasting men was important in giving the Labour Party a new period of strong and stable leadership which was to be of profound importance for the future. As a consequence, therefore, of its undoubted success in office, in marked contrast with the dismal period of the 1930s, the morale of the Labour Party was given a real boost, and its prestige increased in the eyes of the public. Bevin put it to Attlee at the moment of victory in 1945: 'The five years have been a great experience and worthwhile. We have faced many great problems together and have overcome them. One thing it should have done is to remove the inferiority complex among our people' (**113**, ii, 381).

Throughout the war years, however, the Labour Party was also thinking, much more consciously than its Conservative allies, of the postwar world. As early as October 1939 the party had produced its first thoughts on *Labour War Aims*; and this was followed in 1940 by *Labour, the War and the Peace*, and *Labour's Home Policy*, in which it was stated that 'for the Labour Party a Socialist Britain is not some far-off Utopia, but an ideal that can be realised within our time' (**60**, p. 380). Indeed, for Labour the lessons of wartime 'planning', public control and egalitarianism were to be carried over into the postwar world. In *The Old World and the New Society* (1942) these lessons were spelt out more pointedly, and they were driven home in the course of the next two years by the publication of a series of new updated reports on health, education, etc.

All this looked to the future. Some important social legislation, however, was passed even in wartime, mainly as a result of Labour influence and pressure. The means test was ended; allowances and pensions were raised; Bevin's Catering Wages Act aimed at improving conditions in a notoriously backward industry; and Butler's Act of 1944 proved to be a landmark in British educational policy. But on the whole the war period, understandably enough, was one in which the Left had, impatiently, to mark time. Whatever the feeling in the country, the Conservative Party still dominated the House of Commons; and in Churchill they had a leader who had little patience with reforms or panaceas while any of the King's enemies remained in the field, and not very much thereafter. In 1942, when 'Reconstruction' was in the air, he spoke of 'a dangerous optimism . . . growing about post-war conditions' (**27**, p. 170); but, despite his prescience, he could not prevent members of his Government doing something about it. In that same year, as a result of an investigation instituted by Greenwood, Sir William Beveridge produced his famous *Report on the Social Services*, the basis of the postwar Welfare State. Two years later, the Coalition Government in a famous White Paper committed itself to the maintenance of 'Full Employment' after the war. But the piecemeal nature of the Government's programme of social reform, and their refusal to implement important reform proposals immediately, which produced, in a debate on the Beveridge Report, the only anti-government revolt by the Parliamentary Labour Party during the war, disturbed and irritated the backbench members of the Labour Party. It was this that helped to convince them, as the armies of the Allies pushed across Europe, that the Coalition should be brought to an end as soon as possible.

By the spring of 1945, with Allied armies driving towards Berlin from both east and west, the position of Germany was hopeless; and on 7 May the German High Command surrendered unconditionally. With the effective end of the European campaign the question of the Government's future became of immediate political importance. Churchill favoured continuing the Coalition until the end of the war against Japan, though his party advisers, hoping to cash in on Winston's popularity and the euphoria of victory, favoured an immediate election. Herbert Morrison, acting leader of the Labour Party while Attlee was attending the opening sessions of the United Nations Organisation at San Francisco, very sensibly favoured an October election, in order to enable the electoral registers to be brought up to date. But when Attlee returned, he was given the choice by Churchill of either an immediate election or one after the defeat of Japan. Attlee personally supported the latter course; but the Labour Party Conference, then meeting at Blackpool, rejected this notion and plumped for the early election. Churchill thereupon resigned on 23 May as head of the Coalition and formed a 'Caretaker' Government until the result of the general election, to be held on 5 July, was known.

The ex-coalitionists departed on friendly terms; but the mood swiftly changed once the election campaign got under way. The Conservative manifesto was called *Mr Churchill's Declaration of Policy to the Electors*, and it emphasised (as their posters did even more) the need for continuity in government under Churchill's inspired leadership, and 'national' policies; almost as an afterthought a programme of reform measures was tacked on. Labour's programme, *Let Us Face the Future*, made no mention of personalities, but indicated precisely and clearly, what its programme of domestic legislation would be if returned to office: nationalisation, full employment, improved social services, etc. [doc. 26]. It was much hazier, however, than the Conservatives' on international issues. So far as the campaign was concerned, Churchill concluded that the best policy was attack; and in his opening broadcast to the nation of 4 June he argued that the return of a Labour Government would mean a Gestapo-like state: 'A Socialist policy is abhorrent to British ideas of freedom. . . . Socialism is inseparably interwoven with totalitarianism and the abject worship of the State' (56, p. 242). Later Churchill and his chief henchman, Lord Beaverbrook, were able to return to the attack as a result of some indiscreet remarks by Professor Laski, then Chairman of the Labour Party Executive, and argue that the Parliamentary Labour Party and its leader were the creatures of the party's Executive; and indeed, in accordance with the post-1931 revision of the party constitution, there was something in

this. Attlee replied to all these attacks calmly, firmly and sensibly. But
it is doubtful whether these rather absurd exchanges had very much
effect on the electorate. As one parliamentary candidate wrote:

> Abstract questions such as controls versus freedom and complicated
> stories like the Attlee–Laski incident seem terribly far away in the
> streets and factories here. What people want to talk about is
> 'redundancy', housing, pensions and what will happen to ex-
> Servicemen after the war (27, p. 233).

The mood of the electorate was thus quiet, serious and insular;
about seventy-six per cent of those registered voted on 5 July, though,
out of the nearly three million service voters, only about sixty per cent
did so. Since the electoral registers were so out of date and there were
many other imponderables, the politicians were rather in the dark
about the final outcome; though Gallup Poll, exceptionally accurate
albeit unheeded, was available. Churchill told the King that he expected
a majority of 'between thirty and eighty'; the Labour leaders were
rather pessimistic about their chances; and some prophesied a Liberal
revival. In the event, the outcome of the 1945 general election was a
landslide for Labour; and this became apparent as soon as the results
began to flow in on the night of 25 July, the three weeks delay was due
to the need to collect the service vote. On the evening of the following
day, therefore, Churchill resigned, and Attlee accepted the King's
commission to form a new Government, without in fact observing the
niceties of the Labour Party Constitution, as Professor Laski and
Herbert Morrison insisted he should, and obtaining the party's consent
beforehand.

The final outcome was that Labour obtained 393 seats and the
Conservatives 213: the Liberal revival, as so often, failed to materialise,
and they obtained only twelve seats. Labour did not, however, obtain a
majority of the popular vote, and their large number of seats was due to
the inbuilt bias in the electoral system working this time in their favour.
The Labour Party had an overall majority of 146, and thus for the first
time in its history had real power in the House of Commons. 'We are
the masters now!', as a new Labour Minister was supposed to have said.
Moreover, in many respects it was a new party: it represented practically every part of Great Britain; two-thirds of its members had entered
the Commons for the first time and many were youngish professional
men rather than workingmen, the number of trade union members was
now less than a third. The Parliamentary Labour Party was, therefore,
in a real sense a 'national' party; much more so than either its predecessors or, indeed, its Conservative opponents [doc. 27].

How are we to account for this remarkable Labour victory? It is doubtful whether the detailed party programmes or the election campaign itself had much to do with the final result, though the Churchill—Beaverbrook smear campaign against the Labour Party certainly back-fired, and the latter's attack on the prewar record of the Conservative Party was effective enough in its way. Indeed, the backward-looking aspect of the Labour Party's campaign seemed to have fitted in with the mood of the electorate, since, as most historians agree, the party's victory was due primarily to the voters' assessment of the past; it was the Conservatives therefore who were blamed for prewar unemployment, appeasement, and the failure to rearm. *They* were the 'Guilty Men', in the famous yellow-backed squib of that title (by Michael Foot and Mervyn Jones; Gollancz 1957). The Labour Party gained therefore from this revulsion against prewar Conservative policies, and the leftward shift that was its corollary (**66**). The electoral verdict was the result rather than the cause of this radical mood; and, as Pelling suggests, 'the electorate had been showing a persistent bias towards the Left at least since 1942' (**27**, p. 236). Indeed, it is likely that, if the war had not intervened, the Labour Party would have won a general election in 1940. This trend was shown during the war itself by, for example, the successes of the socialist Common Wealth Party — unhampered by the electoral truce — in winning two by-elections and helping to elect a 'progressive' candidate in a third; and in 1943 the Gallup Poll gave Labour a ten per cent lead over its opponents, a result it reiterated in principle on the eve of the 1945 election.

These were negative factors: but the Labour Party also had two positive factors in its favour. First, it had proved itself as a party of government, and could therefore hope to deal effectively with the major issues of domestic policy on which its thinking had concentrated, and in which the electorate was most interested. Secondly, it no longer had any effective challenger on the Left: the Liberals, with only 307 candidates in the field, had no possible chance of forming a government, and the smaller left-wing parties were negligible. The electoral result in 1945 was therefore neither singular nor unexpected. As the authors of the first academic study of that election argue: 'It was the culmination of the long-drawn-out attempt of the Labour party to capture the majority of seats in the House of Commons and to become established in office with the full power of a strongly supported government' (**20**, p. 266).

PART THREE

Assessment

Assessment

'The Labour Party was born out of the bowels of the T.U.C.' Ernest Bevin's pithy remark sums up a mass of writing on the origins of the Labour Party. For though, as we have seen, the revival of socialism in England in the 'eighties and early 'nineties was important and fascinating in terms of ideas and personalities, its direct influence on the birth of the Labour Party (partly because of the persuasive literary gifts of men like Shaw) has been exaggerated. By any reckoning the socialists of the 1890s were a tiny minority, even among trade unionists; and the leaders of the great craft unions were generally bitterly hostile to the socialist creed and strongly committed to supporting the Liberal Party. Moreover, even such support as the socialist societies had managed to build up during this period was waning by the later 'nineties: the twenty-eight candidates of the I.L.P., the socialist group most committed to the formation of an independent Labour Party in Parliament, were utterly trounced at the general election of 1895, and by 1897 'the socialist boom was over' (75).

What led therefore to the formation of the Labour Representation Committee in 1900 was not in any sense the conversion of the British working class, or the trade union movement, to socialism, though it is fair to add that the majority vote at the T.U.C. Congress of 1899 which passed the famous resolution in favour of summoning a special conference 'to devise ways and means' of securing increased labour representation in Parliament, was strongly supported by the socialist-led unions. Rather, the L.R.C. was the result of the trade union movement's belief that, in a period of anti-labour reaction, their ordinary practical trade union aims could best be secured by an increased measure of independent labour representation in the House of Commons. Again, though one must not underestimate the socialist contribution to the formation and development of the Labour Representation Committee, it largely became a trade union pressure group: a point which was driven home when, after the repercussions of Taff Vale, the L.R.C. was rescued from its desperately weak position by a mass insurgence of union affiliations. It was trade union money and support that after 1902 helped to make the L.R.C. a political force in its own right, and thus led to the secret MacDonald—Gladstone pact of the following year. But the twenty-nine L.R.C. members who were then elected in 1906 and formed the new Labour Party, still remained basically representatives of a working-class 'interest' rather than heralds of a new social order. Hence their difficulty in deciding what to do next once the Trades Disputes Act of 1906 had been secured.

Over the reasons for the *formation* of the Labour Party there is now no great disagreement among historians. The reverse is true over the reasons for the *rise* of the Labour Party. The formation of the Labour Party was merely the first step: much more important after 1906 was the question, could the party expand? With hindsight, we know of course that the Labour Party did expand, to oust the Liberal Party, become the second party in the state and eventually achieve real power. But during the decade before the First World War there seemed no inevitability about this process, certainly not to contemporaries. The basic fact about British politics then was the domination of the great Liberal Party. This meant, therefore, that far from expanding as an independent party after 1906 there was a distinct possibility that the Labour Party would be absorbed by the Liberals, as the Liberal Unionists had been by the Conservatives after 1895, or become a small and dwindling left-wing group like the I.L.P. in the 1930s. In the event, partly due to MacDonald's much-maligned leadership, this did not happen and Labour independence was maintained (71). But the ideal of Labour independence implied expansion based on capturing a larger section of the working-class vote: and this could only be done at the expense of liberalism. Hence the relationship between the Liberal and Labour parties during the prewar period (and beyond) is one of the crucial problems in the history of the rise of the Labour Party. Can we already before 1914 discern the beginnings of future Liberal decline and Labour expansion?

A number of historians believe that they can. Indeed, the theme of prewar Liberal decay has until very recently become something of an established orthodoxy, mainly due perhaps to the impressionistic brilliance of George Dangerfield's *The Strange Death of Liberal England* (1935). Dangerfield's thesis has been given a partial and more scholarly justification by the writings of recent historians like Henry Pelling and Paul Thompson. Thompson, in his study of London politics between 1885 and 1914 has pointed to the financial and organisational weaknesses of the Liberal Party up to 1906; its failures in local elections ('the Liberal Party was rotting at its roots'); its continuing links with middle-class nonconformist ambitions; and its general inability to adapt itself to working-class needs and aspirations. Hence the Conservative domination of London in the later nineteenth century. Even the Liberal victory of 1906 was, he argues, not a genuine revival, but the result of a number of special, though ephemeral, advantages gained by the Liberals as a result of the unpopularity of Conservative policies. 'The recovery of the nineteen-hundreds', he writes, 'gave a deceptive illusion of strength, for it was not based on the solution of the Liberal Party's real problems. It still lacked a firm working-class basis, a secure financial backing and a coherent political standpoint' (**80**, p. 189). This view has been reinforced by the attitude of Bealey and Pelling towards the election of 1906, which they see not as a profound demand for a 'new' liberalism of social reform and increased state activity, but of a hankering after the old — elected school boards and free trade — a viewpoint which fits in well with Pelling's own scepticism about the reality of working-class demands for state-sponsored social reforms during this period (**54**; **26**, ch. 1).

The corollary of prewar Liberal weakness is, potentially at least, Labour strength; and Pelling and others, while not denying the evident weaknesses of the Labour Party during these years, have stressed (in the words of Dr Gregory in his study of the miners and politics) 'the strength of the roots put down before 1914' (**90**, p. 178). Pelling, for example, has emphasised repeatedly the enormous importance of increasing trade union affiliations for future Labour development (**26**, ch. 6); and especially the accession of the Miners' Federation of Great Britain in 1909, which at one stroke increased party membership in the House of Commons by fifteen, and held out the alluring prospect of all the miners' pocket boroughs being swept into the Labour net, as indeed they were after 1918. Moreover, he stresses the importance of those more general social and economic factors — growing difficulties in basic industries like coal, for example, coupled with increasing geographical unity on the one hand but deeper class divisions on the other — which were bound eventually to play into the hands of the Labour Party (**26**, ch. 6). Dr Gregory has illustrated in detail the importance of these factors for the prospects of the party in the coalfields between 1906 and 1914 (**90**). By the eve of the First World War, as he points out, the Liberal alliance was already beginning to crumble, and the M.F.G.B. was proposing to sponsor twenty-one Labour candidates against the Liberals at the next election. Indeed, one recent estimate suggests that the Labour Party would then have put up between 150 and 170 candidates, compared with seventy-eight, the highest number previously (**71**). In one way or another, therefore, the conditions were being prepared for Labour's great leap forward in the postwar world. The Liberal Party was doomed.

It is this whole thesis of the inexorability of the Labour advance that was rejected by Professor Trevor Wilson in the preface to his book on the Liberal Party after 1914. He sees the great Liberal victory of 1906 as the beginning of a new period of Liberal revival which, based on an increased working-class vote and the solid legislative achievements of the next six years, would have been sustained if it had not been for the disastrous divisions created by the First World War (**31**). But since his primary concern was with the period after 1914, Professor Wilson's criticisms were based on no detailed research into the prewar period. This has now been remedied by the work of P. F. Clarke in *Lancashire and the New Liberalism* (**10**). Dr Clarke argues that the Liberal Party, as evidenced particularly by the elections of 1906 and 1910, was in fact building up strong support among the working class in the great industrial cities during the whole Edwardian period; not only in Lancashire, but even (*pace* Dr Thompson) in London. This was so, he suggests, *after* the emergence of 'class politics' − i.e. working-class recognition of the primacy of economic and social issues − in the first decade of the century, a process more or less completed by and reflected in the elections of 1910. The workers' recognition of their 'class' position thus drove them not away from but towards the Liberal Party.

Why was this? Dr Clarke suggests that in the early twentieth century there *was* a genuine Liberal revival, linked with opposition to the Boer War and Conservative reaction, and based on the ethic of 'Progressivism': social reform and anti-Imperialism, fostered by national party organisation. This 'New Liberalism' was supported by statesmen of inspiration and genius, including Churchill and Lloyd George, and sustained, ideologically, by the circle around C. P. Scott of the *Manchester Guardian*. 'The Liberal revival', he writes, 'gave evidence of its scale in 1906 and its durability in 1910' (**10**, p. 151); and there was no reason to believe that it would not continue among the working class. The Labour Party can best be seen, therefore, argues Dr Clarke, as a part, but only a part, of the Edwardian Progressive Movement. Conceived as an *independent* political party, it was narrow, weak, uninspired, and irrelevant, for the Liberals could have retained power in 1910 with Irish votes alone. Labour electoral history during these years (even apart from the dismal condition of the Parliamentary party) gives much substance to these views. In twenty of the twenty-four seats where Labour opposed Liberal candidates in January 1910, Labour finished bottom of the poll; Labour was bottom of the poll again in all the fourteen by-elections they fought between December 1910 and July 1914, though Henry Pelling has argued that nevertheless in terms of votes Labour was still doing better than this indicates (**26**, ch. 6).

In principle, there is no necessary incompatibility between the views of the two groups of historians, since they differ not so much over the facts but rather over the time scale into which those facts should be fitted. Looked at from the point of view of pre-1914, Professor Wilson and Dr Clarke are right to stress the weaknesses of the Labour position; on the other hand, Henry Pelling's insistence on the importance of those fundamental social and economic factors which in the long run were likely to benefit the Labour Party, seems equally valid. In particular, his emphasis on the key importance of growing trade union links with Labour (seen so powerfully during the First World War) seems persistently underrated by 'pro-Liberal' historians, though it is important to remember of course that a trade unionist did not necessarily vote Labour merely because his union had affiliated to the Labour Party! The trouble is that it is so difficult to isolate the effects of such long-term factors from the more immediate and obvious impact of political events; and at the heart of this controversy is a political event of major importance: the Liberal split during the First World War. The consequences of this split in helping the Labour Party to dislodge the Liberal Party (as revealed in the electoral statistics 1918-24) have seemed so profound to many historians as to render otiose squabbles over the prewar positions of the two parties.

Nevertheless, even the immediate postwar period of Liberal 'downfall' no longer seems quite as inevitable as once it did. After 1918 the Labour Party at last (as Maurice Cowling argues) 'broke through the dams which the Liberal Party had built' and entered, with evident satisfaction, the world of 'high politics' **(61)**. He also reminds us, however, in his analysis of the politics of these years, how fluid the political situation then was; with a three (or four?)-party system operating within an electorate which had swelled enormously since 1914, and many of whose members (including of course women over thirty) had had no experience of voting before. The Liberal decline was therefore, he suggests, 'a more contingent matter than the (electoral) statistics suggest and was not contained in the prewar situation' **(61, p. 420)**. A similar point has been made by Chris Cooke with particular reference to the 1923 election. Though the Liberal Party was clearly in decline in the five years after the Armistice, he sees a real 'Liberal revival' in that year (when the party was reunited under Asquith and Lloyd George) based on the rural constituencies; and indeed the voting figures for the Liberal and Labour parties in that election were very close (Labour: 4,438,508; Liberal: 4,311,147). But these new Liberal advantages were thrown away, principally by the disastrous mistakes of the party leaders in their dealings with the Labour Party and the first

Labour Government. The result was seen at the general election of 1924 when the number of Liberals in the House dropped from 159 to 42! 'The Liberal revival of 1923', writes Mr Cooke, 'had become the disaster of 1924. The decline of the party had been transformed into its downfall, not by any "inevitable" historical process, but in the last resort, by a succession of accidents' (11, p. 313).

After 1924 the Labour Party had once and for all displaced the Liberal Party as the second party in the state, and therefore became the only possible alternative government to the Conservatives. This was still true in the 1930s despite the failures of the second Labour Government and the crisis of 1931. It was then that the Labour Party under new leaders and facing new problems slowly and painfully rebuilt itself, though, as the results of the 1935 general election showed, the country was not yet ready to grant the party real power. That election, by eliminating the Liberals almost completely as an effective force in British politics, at last brought to an end the peculiar love—hate relationship between the two radical parties that had lasted since 1900, and marked the return once again to two-party politics. Henceforth the struggle for power would be between the Labour and the Conservative parties. These verdicts were confirmed by the experience of the Second World War, and the general election of 1945. The great electoral victory of that year effectively begins, therefore, a new period in the history of the Labour Party, and the life of the nation.

PART FOUR

Documents

Henry George on 'landlordism'

In Progress and Poverty *Henry George argued, as below, that the land-lord through his control of rent held the community up to ransom. The remedy for this was for the state to impose a 'Single Tax' on land. This proposal had no practical effect; but George's onslaught on private property and the inequalities it produced, had a powerful influence on English socialists in the 1880s.*

Look over the world to-day. In countries the most widely differing — under conditions the most diverse as to government, as to industries, as to tariffs, as to currency — you will find distress among the working classes; but everywhere that you thus find distress and destitution in the midst of wealth, you will find that the land is monopolised; that instead of being treated as the common property of the whole people it is treated as the private property of individuals; that for its use by labour large revenues are extorted from the earnings of labour. Look over the world to-day, comparing different countries with each other, and you will see that it is not the abundance of capital or the productiveness of labour that makes wages high or low; but the extent to which the monopolizers of land can, in rent, levy tribute upon the earnings of labour. . . . As land increases in value, poverty deepens and pauperism appears. In the new settlements, where land is cheap, you will find no beggars and inequalities in condition are very slight. In the great cities, where land is so valuable that it is measured by the foot, you will find the extremes of poverty and luxury. . . .

From *Progress and Poverty*, Kegan Paul, 1883 edn, pp. 203-4.

William Morris on socialism

The following extract shows why a wealthy middle-class Englishman, who was also a great creative artist, abandoned radicalism for socialism, and joined the S.D.F. in 1883. It also provides a further glimpse of the influence of Henry George.

I should have been glad to have continued our conversation last Friday night; as I so much desire to convert all disinterested people of good will to what I should call active and general Socialism, and to have their help: I think that you, like myself, have really been a Socialist for a long time, and I know you have done your best, as you would be sure to do, to carry out your views. For my part I used to think that one might further real Socialistic progress by doing what one could on the lines of ordinary middle-class Radicalism: I have been driven of late into the conclusion that I was mistaken; that Radicalism is on the wrong line, so to say, and will never develop into anything more than Radicalism: in fact that it is made for and by the middle classes and will always be under the control of rich capitalists: they will have no objection to its *political* development, if they think they can stop it there: but as to real social changes, they will not allow them if they can help it: you may see almost any day such phrases as "this is the proper way to stop the spread of Socialism" in the Liberal papers, the writer of the phrase never having taken the trouble to find out what Socialism meant, and also choosing to ignore the discontent, dumb indeed for the most part, which is widely spread in England. Meantime I can see no use in people having political freedom unless they use it as an instrument for leading reasonable and manlike lives; no good even in education if, when they are educated, people have only slavish work to do, and have to live lives too much beset with sordid anxiety for them to be able to think and feel with the more fortunate people who produced art and poetry and great thought. This release from slavery it is clear cannot come to people so long as they are subjected to the bare subsistence wages which are a necessity for competitive commerce: and I cannot help thinking that the workmen will be soon finding out that for themselves: it is certain that Henry George's book has been received in this country and in America as a new Gospel.

William Morris to C. E. Maurice, 22 June 1883 (**123**, pp. 173-4).

document 3

Tom Mann on Hyndman

Tom Mann was a young skilled engineer who joined the S.D.F. in the

1880s. His Memoirs *provide a vivid picture of labour activities in the later nineteenth century. His restless temperament drove him from one militant movement to another during his long life; he ended up in the British Communist Party.*

Hyndman was a very different personality. In the early days of open-air propaganda — for he took his turn regularly at outdoor gatherings as well as indoor — his essentially bourgeois appearance attracted much attention. The tall hat, the frock coat, and the long beard often drew the curious-minded who would not have spent time listening to one in workman's attire. Hyndman always gave the unadulterated Social Democratic doctrine, as propounded by the Social Democratic Federation. He never whittled down his revolutionary principles, or expressed them in sugar-coated phrases. He took the greatest delight in exposing the exploitation carried on by the capitalists, and especially by those who championed Liberal and Radical principles, and were thought highly of by the workmen members of Radical clubs. He cleverly criticised the workmen listening to him for not being able to see through the machinations of those members of the master class, closely associated with the church or politics, or both. At almost every meeting he addressed, Hyndman would cynically thank the audience for so 'generously supporting my class'. Indeed, he brought in 'my class' to an objectionable degree. It seemed to some of us that it would have been better if he could have dropped this reference, but none of us doubted his whole-souled advocacy of Socialism as he conceived it. Hyndman, like many strong personalities, had very pronounced likes and dislikes. To myself, he was ever kind and courteous. I am quite sure he did much valuable work at the particular time when that special work was needed.

It was no small matter to know that in our advocacy of the principles we had learned to love, which on so many occasions brought forth stinging criticisms from the press, Hyndman's ability to state the case comprehensively, logically, and argumentatively, was at our disposal always, and was of very great value indeed. I am convinced, however, that Hyndman's bourgeois mentality made it impossible for him to estimate the worth of industrial organisation correctly. For many years he attached no importance whatever to the trade-union movement, and his influence told disastrously on others.

(**126**, pp. 26-7.)

document 4
'Bloody Sunday'

'Bloody Sunday', 13 November 1887, was the culmination of the attempt by radicals and socialists to fight for free speech in London, by staging a demonstration in Trafalgar Square. It was banned and broken up by the police. Graham and Burns each received six weeks imprisonment for their part in the affray.

The contingents from Rotherhithe, Bermondsey and the South-Eastern Division consisted of fully 20,000 persons . . . at four o'clock the processions from Peckham, Bermondsey, Deptford and Battersea made their appearance at the Westminster end of the bridge. . . . Superintendent Dunlop then gave orders to his men to disperse the assembly. . . . Borne by members of the procession were about 15 banners and for these the police made. . . . During the melee, the police freely used their weapons, and the people, who were armed with iron bars, pokers, gaspipes and short sticks, and even knives, resisted them in a most determined manner. . . . A similar scene was being enacted in the Strand at the corner of Wellington Street. . . .

A minute or so after four o'clock, which was the hour announced for the meeting to take place, six waggonettes, heavily laden with passengers, and having in the leading vehicle a brass band and two red flags, approached the square from Shaftesbury Avenue. Almost at the same instant about one hundred persons crossed from the footpath in front of Morley's Hotel, as if to enter the square. Mr J. Cunninghame-Graham, M.P., John Burns, the Socialist, Mrs Besant, and others were in this group. Sticks were flourished in the air, and a most resolute rush was made to break through the cordon of police, who stood four deep. The crowd had all but succeeded in penetrating through the police ranks when the reserves inside the square rallied to the support of the main body and a score of police troopers charged pell-mell into the fray. Sticks and batons swished through the air, hats went flying. Several arrests were in this instance made by the police, their chief captures being those of Mr C. Graham, M.P., and Mr John Burns, who were carried into the middle of the square, and kept in custody there for some little time.

From *Reynolds' Newspaper*, 20 November 1887.

Shaw on the Fabians

document 5

The following is part of a letter describing, in Bernard Shaw's inimitable style, the early Fabians and the aims and ethos of the Fabian Society.

The Fabians are not the property of a single rich man, like the [Socialist] League; and they never get into trouble by disorderly behaviour or require defence funds. The statements put forward by the Fabians have never been denied or refuted. They have never lied about their own strength. When any difficult work has been on hand — when a 70 guinea conference with the radicals and secularists has been needed — when an opponent for Bradlaugh has been desiderated — when answers to really scientific champions have been required by the Commonweal — when, in short, sensible and educated workers who mean business, either as lecturers or writers, have been indispensable — then have the braggarts turned to the Fabian for help, and have gotten it in a noble oblivion of insult and disparagement. The Fabian lecturers are famous throughout the world. Their women are beautiful; their men brave. Their executive council challenges the universe for quality, comprising as it does the eyeglassed and indomitable Bland (treasurer of the society — editor of To-Day, which is renowned for its poetry — verb. sap.), the provenly heroic Annie Besant, the blameless Shaw, a genuine working man [W. L. Phillips] in the lath & plaster line, and three other men of approved distinction and fiery devotion — the least of them an M.A. Join the Fabian, and you will find its name a puissant protector.

G. B. Shaw to Pakenham Beatty, 27 May 1887 (**125**, pp. 169-70).

The Fabian programme 1886

The Fabian Society consists of Socialists.

It therefore aims at the reorganisation of Society by the emancipation of Land and Industrial Capital from individual and class ownership, and the vesting of them in the community for the general benefit. In this way only can the natural and acquired advantages of the country be equitably shared by the whole people.

The Society accordingly works for the extinction of private property in Land and of the consequent individual appropriation, in the form of Rent, of the price paid for permission to use the earth, as well as for the advantages of superior soils and sites.

The Society, further, works for the transfer to the community of the administration of such industrial Capital as can conveniently be managed socially. For, owing to the monopoly of the means of production in the past, industrial inventions and the transformation of surplus income into Capital have mainly enriched the proprietary class, the worker being now dependent on that class for leave to earn a living.

. If these measures be carried out, without compensation (though not without such relief to expropriated individuals as may seem fit to the community), Rent and Interest will be added to the reward of labour, the idle class now living on the labour of others will necessarily disappear, and practical equality of opportunity will be maintained by the spontaneous action of economic forces with much less interference with personal liberty than the present system entails.

For the attainment of these ends the Fabian Society looks to the spread of Socialist opinions, and the social and political changes consequent thereon. It seeks to achieve these ends by the general dissemination of knowledge as to the relation between the individual and Society in its economic, ethical, and political aspects.

(46, p. 284.)

The 'inevitability of gradualness'

This extract from Sidney Webb's 'The historic basis of Socialism' in Fabian Essays (1889), well illustrates the Fabian commitment to the 'inevitability of gradualness' — slow, peaceful democratic change leading to Socialism.

In the present Socialist movement these two streams are united: advocates of social reconstruction have learnt the lesson of Democracy, and know that it is through the slow and gradual turning of the popular mind to new principles that social reorganization bit by bit comes. All students of society who are abreast of their time, Socialists as well as Individualists, realize that important organic changes can only be (1) democratic, and thus acceptable to a majority of the people, and prepared for in the minds of all; (2) gradual, and thus causing no dislocation, however rapid may be the rate of progress; (3) not regarded as immoral by the mass of the people, and thus not subjectively demoralizing to them; and (4) in this country at any rate, constitutional and peaceful. Socialists may therefore be quite at one with Radicals in their political methods. Radicals, on the other hand, are perforce realizing that mere political levelling is insufficient to save a State from anarchy and despair. Both sections have been driven to recognize that the root of the difficulty is economic; and there is every day a wider consensus that the inevitable outcome of Democracy is the control by the people themselves, not only of their own political organization, but, through that, also of the main instruments of wealth production; the gradual substitution of organized co-operation for the anarchy of the competitive struggle; and the consequent recovery, in the only possible way, of what John Stuart Mill calls 'the enormous share which the possessors of the instruments of industry are able to take from the produce'. The economic side of the democratic ideal is, in fact, Socialism itself.

(**37**, pp. 32-3.)

The Gas Workers' Union 1889

Will Thorne describes, in the extract below, how he founded the Gas Workers' Union at the Beckton Works in East London in 1889. The workers demanded and gained without a struggle the eight hour day. This is one of the great moments in the history of new unionism – the organisation of trade unions among unskilled workers, and was followed a few months later by the Great Dock Strike.

The time of the formation of a union was approaching rapidly. It was precipitated by the introduction of a practice by which the stage foremen would come to certain men on Sunday morning and order them to stay on to do three extra charges. This meant that, instead of finishing at 5.30, the men had to work right through until ten or eleven o'clock.

Generally the men had no food, because when they left home they did not know that they would have to stay on and work later. There was a big canteen adjacent to the works, where sometimes food and drink were obtainable, but when the eighteen-hour shift was finished, the men living at Poplar and Canning Town, as most of them did, had a walk of nearly four miles. This caused a great deal of annoyance and, on top of the other slave-driving methods, caused the men to get desperate. They were almost prepared to go on strike, even though they had no union behind them. I saw the time was ripe; the day that I had waited for so long had at last dawned. This was the psychological moment for forming the union.

A few of us got together; I gave them my views, and we held a meeting. This was on March 31st, 1889. The meeting was held at the present site of the Canning Town Public Hall.

A resolution was passed in favour of a gas workers' union being formed, with the eight-hour day as one of its objects. With George Angle and George Gilby, I was elected as a delegate to represent my shift. The opposite shift was represented by four other men, Hutchings, Mack, Gundy, and Mansfield – God bless their brave hearts!

Prior to the meeting we interviewed all the men in the different parts of the works, and asked them if they were in favour of a union being established at Beckton without pledging themselves to join it. The answers were very favourable.

Sunday morning, March 31st, 1889 — a lovely sunny morning — was the birthday of the National Union of Gas Workers and General Labourers of Great Britain and Ireland. To-day it is the largest union of its kind in the world.

From Will Thorne, *My Life's Battles* (**135**, pp. 66-7).

document 9

The Great Dock Strike 1889

The following account, from the classic contemporary study of the dispute by H. Llewellyn Smith and Vaughan Nash, describes the early days of the Great Dock Strike.

But the weather, like everything else, seemed to have been pressed into the dockers' cause, and the sun shone down brilliantly from a cloudless August sky that morning on a vast congregation of upturned faces, stretching from the East India Dock gates across the roadway to the pavement beyond. Thousands of men were there — seedy dockers and sturdy stevedores, sailors and firemen, in the fresh enthusiasm of their new trade union, weather-stained lightermen, and coalies cleaned up for Sunday — all branches, in short, of riverside labour; and on the outskirts of the crowd stood not a few engineers and other skilled artisans ready to show their sympathy with the revolt of unskilled labour. All eyes were turned towards the wagon drawn up in front of the closed dock gates, and the extemporised platform was eagerly scanned for the white straw hat, but John Burns was away at Battersea, and it was Ben Tillett's high-pitched but far-reaching voice that first addressed the meeting. A movement in the crowd, a cry of 'make way', a shifting among the occupants of the wagon, and Tom Mann pressed his way to the front. . . .

It is a great throng that is gathering, though nothing to the huge numbers reached in later stages of the strike. Thousands of dockers are there, chiefly from the East and West India Docks, and thousands more of stevedores, whose banners add colour to the crowd. There are in all forty banners of trade and friendly societies; and fish-heads, onions, and tiny loaves are carried on pikes as an object-lesson in dockers' fare to the magnates of the city. The forty banners are soon increased to forty-one, as a body of three hundred Millwall men — the first contingent from the grain and timber docks — march up, amid general cheering, with a pink rag fluttering from a pole. Swelled by the addition of two or three thousand men from the London and St. Katharine Docks, the miscellaneous crowd make the customary tour of the narrow city streets, chaffing the police, and groaning at the Dock House as they pass.

Many processions on other days were larger and more imposing, but it was this Monday's demonstration which first thoroughly aroused the City to the fact that something unusual was going forward in the unknown country to the east of Aldgate pump.

From H. Llewellyn Smith and Vaughan Nash, *The Story of the Dockers' Strike* (**108**, pp. 59-65).

document 10

New Unionism

Mann and Tillett (together with John Burns) were the main leaders of the Great Dock Strike 1889; and, in the 1890s, two of the leading protagonists of the New Unionism whose ethos is illustrated below.

In conclusion, we repeat that the real difference between the 'new' and the 'old' is, that those who belong to the latter, and delight in being distinct from the policy endorsed by the 'new', do so because they do not recognise, as we do, that it is the work of *the trade unionist to stamp out poverty from the land.* They do not contend, as we contend, that existing unions should exert themselves to extend organisations where they as yet do not exist. They know the enormous difficulties under which hundreds of thousands labour, and how difficult it is for them to take the initial steps in genuine trades unionism and how valuable a little 'coaching' would be from those who have had experience in such matters; but they have not done what they might to supply this — we shall. A new enthusiasm is required, a fervent zeal that will result in the sending forth of trade union organisers as missionaries through the length and breadth of the country.

Clannishness in trade matters must be superseded by a cosmopolitan spirit, brotherhood must not only be talked of but practised; and that real grit exists in the 'new' unions is evident, not only from the manner in which they are perfecting their own organisations, but also from the substantial way in which they have contributed to the support of other trades, such as the bargebuilders, whose strike balance-sheet shows that the 'new' unions were much more prompt in rendering monetary aid than the 'old' ones. Nevertheless, what we desire to see is a unification of all, a dropping of all bickerings, and an earnest devotion to duty taking the place of the old indifference. The cause we have at heart is too sacred to admit of time being spent quarrelling amongst ourselves, and whilst we make no pretence to the possession of special virtues, we are prepared to work unceasingly for the economic emancipation of the workers. Our ideal *is a Co-operative Commonwealth.*

From Tom Mann and Ben Tillett, *The 'New' Trades Unionism* (**99**, p. 15).

The Red Flag

document 11

The 'Red Flag' was written in 1889 by Jim Connell, the Irish socialist, in memory of the European socialist dead. Sung to a mournful German tune (which Connell detested) it has always been associated with British Labour gatherings.

> The people's flag is deepest red,
> It shrouded oft our martyred dead,
> And ere their limbs grew stiff or cold,
> Their heart's blood dyed its every fold.
>
>   *   *   *
>
> With heads uncovered swear we all,
> To bear it onward till we fall,
> Come dungeon dark, or gallows grim,
> This song shall be our parting hymn.
>
> Then raise the scarlet standard high!
> Within its shade we'll live and die.
> Though cowards flinch and traitors sneer,
> We'll keep the Red Flag flying here.

Keir Hardie as M.P.

Keir Hardie, who was returned as Labour M.P. for West Ham in 1892, refused – unlike his fellow labour members – to toe the Liberal Party line, and insisted on asserting his independence. Here he justifies his position to his constituents.

'The I.L.P.', he said, 'starts from the assumption that the worker should be as free industrially and economically as he is supposed to be politically, that the land and the instruments of production should be owned by the community and should be used in producing the requisites to maintain a healthy and happy existence. The men who are to achieve these reforms must be under no obligation whatever to either the landlord or the capitalist, or to any party or organisation representing these interests. Suppose, for the sake of argument, that twenty members would be returned to Parliament who were nominally Labour Members but who owed their election to a compromise with the Liberals, what would the effect be upon their action in the House of Commons? When questions affecting the interest of property were at stake, or when they desired to take action to compel social legislation of a drastic character, the threat would be always hanging over them that unless they were obedient to the party Whip and maintained party discipline they would be opposed. In my own case, this threat has been held out so often that it is beginning to lose its effect. I have no desire to hold the seat on sufferance and at the mercy of those who are not in agreement with me, and am quite prepared to be defeated when the election comes round. But I cannot agree to compromise my independence of action in even the slightest degree'.

From William Stewart, *J. Keir Hardie* (**133**, pp. 90-1).

The early I.L.P.

The young Philip Snowden early became an active and outstanding member of the Independent Labour Party in Yorkshire. The following extract from his Autobiography *describes the work of these enthusiasts – a far cry from Snowden's later grim years as Labour Chancellor.*

The Party quickly developed a large number of local speakers. Many young men who were Nonconformist local preachers were attracted to the movement by the ethical appeal of Socialism. Their experience in speaking was a great help to the Party propaganda. Working men who had toiled all day at arduous work went out at nights into the streets to preach in their simple way the new gospel of emancipation. Men who had never before attempted public speaking were given courage and the gift of effective oratory by the new passion for social justice which consumed them. The movement was something new in politics. It was politics inspired by idealism and religious fervour. Vocal Unions were formed which accompanied cycling corps into the country at weekends, and audiences were gathered on village greens by the singing of the choirs; then short and simple addresses on Socialism were given. On their country jaunts the cyclists distributed leaflets and pasted slips on gates, and sometimes stuck them on cows, bearing such slogans as 'Socialism the Hope of the World', 'Workers of the World Unite'. Sometimes processions were organised in connection with a meeting of more than usual importance addressed by some national speaker. I remember one such procession where the small children were on a horse-drawn lorry, and stretched across the wagon over their heads was a banner bearing the Socialist slogan 'Production for Use and not for Profit!'

From Philip Snowden, *An Autobiography* (**132**, i, 71).

'Merrie England'

document 14

Robert Blatchford, a journalist of genius and editor of Clarion, *published in* Merrie England *(1895) one of the few socialist best-sellers. His rather endearing conception of Socialism is well illustrated in the following extract.*

So now let me tell you roughly what I suggest as an improvement on things as they now are.

First of all I would set men to work to grow wheat and fruit and rear cattle and poultry for our own use. Then I would develop the fisheries and construct great fish-breeding lakes and harbours. Then I would restrict our mines, furnaces, chemical works, and factories to the number actually needed for the supply of our own people. Then I would stop the smoke nuisance by developing water power and electricity.

In order to achieve these ends I would make all the land, mills, mines, factories, works, shops, ships, and railways the property of the people.

I would have the towns rebuilt with wide streets, with detached houses, with gardens and fountains and avenues of trees. I would make the railways, the carriage of letters, and the transit of goods as free as the roads and bridges.

I would make the houses loftier and larger, and clear them of all useless furniture. I would institute public dining halls, public baths, public wash-houses on the best plans, and so set free the hands of those slaves — our English women.

I would have public parks, public theatres, music halls, gymnasiums, football and cricket fields, public halls and public gardens for recreation and music and refreshment. I would have all our children fed and clothed and educated at the cost of the State. I would have them all taught to play and to sing. I would have them all trained to athletics and to arms. I would have public halls of science. I would have the people become their own artists, actors, musicians, soldiers, and police. Then, by degrees I would make all these things *free*. So that clothing, lodging, fuel, food, amusement, intercourse, education, and all the requirements for a perfect human life should be produced and distributed and enjoyed by the people without the use of money.

Now, Mr. John Smith, practical and hard-headed man, look upon the two pictures. You may think that mine represents a state of things that is unattainable; but you *must* own that it is much fairer than the picture of things as they are.

As to the possibility of doing what I suggest, we will consider all that in a future chapter. At present ask yourself two questions:—

1. Is Modern England as happy as it might be?
2. Is *my* England — Merrie England — a better place than the England in which we now live?

From Robert Blatchford, *Merrie England* (33, pp. 43-4).

The Liberal-Labour electoral pact 1903

In order to prevent rivalry between Labour and Liberal candidates at the next general election, both sides began to consider the possibility of an 'electoral pact'. Here, Jesse Herbert, Herbert Gladstone's secretary, writes to the Liberal Chief Whip suggesting the advantages to the Liberal Party of such an arrangement. It was finally concluded (secretly) between Gladstone and Ramsay MacDonald in August 1903.

A determination of the course to be followed by the Liberal party is urgently needed, for to do nothing is to seem to reject the overtures of the L.R.C., who may be irretrievably committed to courses during delay which they would avoid if they anticipated future friendly relations.

I am keenly conscious that the matter is not so simple and clear that it may be determined in the off-hand manner in which it is dealt with by many Liberals as well as Labour men. The official recognition of a separate group unpledged to support of the Liberal party, a group which will harrass every Government and whose representatives in Parliament will probably decline the Liberal whip, is not lightly to be given. It would be the recognition of a vital change in the organization of parties. But would it be other than the official recognition of a fact, indisputable, and clear to every individual politician? There is no difficulty experienced in giving official recognition to the League group which has wealth. Why should there be difficulty in giving official recognition to the Labour group which has numbers? Neither asks for an official approval of its objects, but both seek the friendly concession by the party of the liberty to run their candidates unhampered by the presence of official candidates.

Are the principles and objects of the L.R.C. such as to justify such a benevolent attitude? Will the success of the Liberal party at the polls be too dearly purchased at the price? Ought the Liberal party to prefer defeat rather than assist in any way to foster the growing power of the Labour Party?

These are questions the answers to which necessitate an excursus into a political discussion which it would be presumptuous of one to make. I am concerned with the electoral prospects of the party, and anxiously ask myself, 'What would be the gain and the loss to the party at the General Election, if a working arrangement were arrived at with the L.R.C.?' There are some members of the party in and out of Parliament who would be estranged thereby, but they are few. Those employers of labour who remained with the Liberal party when the Whig seceders went out on the Home Rule excuse, have (with few exceptions) sincere sympathy with many of the objects of the L.R.C. The severe Individualists of the party who are wholly out of sympathy with the principles of the L.R.C. are very few. The total loss of their financial aid and of their votes would be inconsiderable. The gain to the party through a working arrangement would be great, and can be measured best by a comparison of the results of 'no arrangement' with those of 'an arrangement'.

The L.R.C. can directly influence the votes of nearly a million men. They will have a fighting fund of £100,000. (This is the most significant new fact in the situation. Labour candidates have had hitherto to beg for financial help, and have fought with paltry and wholly insufficient funds.) Their members are mainly men who have hitherto voted with the Liberal Party. Should they be advised to vote against Liberal candidates, and (as they probably would) should they act as advised, the Liberal party would suffer defeat not only in those constituencies where L.R.C. candidates fought, but also in almost every borough, and in many of the Divisions of Lancashire and Yorkshire. This would be the inevitable result of unfriendly action towards the L.R.C. candidates. They would be defeated, but so also should we be defeated.

If there be good-fellowship between us and the L.R.C. the aspect of the future for both will be very bright and encouraging.

Jesse Herbert to Herbert Gladstone, 6 March 1903 (**53**, pp. 265-6).

document 16

The Labour electoral manifesto 1906

This shows the moderateness of the Labour programme, and its similarity to that of the Liberals.

To the Electors —

This election is to decide whether or not Labour is to be fairly represented in Parliament.

The House of Commons is supposed to be the people's House, and yet the people are not there.

Landlords, employers, lawyers, brewers, and financiers are there in force. Why not Labour?

The Trade Unions ask the same liberty as capital enjoys. They are refused.

The aged poor are neglected.

The slums remain; overcrowding continues, whilst the land goes to waste.

Shopkeepers and traders are overburdened with rates and taxation, whilst the increasing land values, which should relieve the ratepayers, go to people who have not earned them.

Wars are fought to make the rich richer, and underfed school children are still neglected.

Chinese Labour is defended because it enriches the mine owners.

The unemployed ask for work, the Government gave them a worthless Act, and now, when you are beginning to understand the causes of your poverty, the red herring of Protection is drawn across your path.

Protection, as experience shows, is no remedy for poverty and unemployment. It serves to keep you from dealing with the land, housing, old age, and other social problems!

You have it in your power to see that Parliament carries out your wishes. The Labour Representation Executive appeals to you in the name of a million Trade Unionists to forget all the political differences which have kept you apart in the past, and vote for —— (here is inserted the name of the Labour candidate).

(54, pp. 264-5.)

document 17

The Parliamentary Labour Party before 1914

The following two extracts illustrate independent socialist views of the pre-1914 Parliamentary Labour Party. The first, by Ben Tillett, shows left-wing disquiet at the moderateness of the party leadership and their truckling to the Liberal Party — especially over questions like temperance reform. The second, by Beatrice Webb, shows the growing disillusionment over the party's record by 1914.

[a] The House of Commons and the country, which respected and feared the Labour Party, are now fast approaching a condition of contempt towards its Parliamentary representatives.

The lion has no teeth or claws, and is losing his growl, too; the temperance section being softly feline in their purring to Ministers and their patronage. Those of the Party, who, out of a sense of loyalty to others, refrain from protest, indicate more patience than courage in their attitude. . . .

Labour is robbed of the wealth and means of life created by the genius of toil; the exploiters are on trial for their malefactions; the charge is that capitalist ownership of the land and material wealth is the cause of poverty. When that has been sufficiently explained and taught the people, there will be ample time for side issues, after the real work is done. I do not hesitate to describe the conduct of these blind leaders as nothing short of betrayal especially with the fact in view that they have displayed greater activity for temperance reform than for Labour interests. Of all the farces, these same Labour-Temperance advocates knew the Bill would never pass the House of Lords; if not, they are not merely innocent but they are ignorant of their business, and cannot see an inch before their noses. Every Labour man knew the attitude of the Lords; all the Liberals did, for the game was played with the cards on the table. What a mockery it was, and merely to waste time. While Shackleton took the chair for Winston Churchill, thousands of textile workers were suffering starvation through unemployment; his ability and energy could have been well used in Stevenson Square, in Manchester, instead of mouthing platitudes and piffle in Liberal meetings. The worst of the winter is coming on, time thrown away will never be recovered, and thousands will perish for want of bread. A great many of the victims to destitution will be in their graves before the Liberal Government will have approached the subject of unemployment, which they will sandwich between abolition of the House of Lords and Welsh Disestablishment. The temperance section, in particular, will be seizing on the other 'red-herrings', and the winter will have passed, and these unctuous weaklings will go on prattling their nonsense, the while thousands are dying of starvation. Some of these lives might have been saved to the country, the misery consequent to foodless conditions of life averted. Blessed, valuable months have been lost; the Labour movement must not tolerate the further betrayal of interests with agitations about the House of Lords, or Welsh Disestablishment.

From Ben Tillett, *Is the Parliamentary Labour Party a failure?* London 1908, pp. 11-15.

[b] We attended the Gala days of the I.L.P. conference (the twenty-first anniversary of its existence) as fraternal delegates from the Fabian Society, and listened to endless self-congratulatory speeches from I.L.P. leaders and a fine piece of oratory from Huysmans — a man of far finer calibre than our British leaders. When the conference settled down to business the I.L.P. leaders were painfully at variance. J. R. MacDonald seems almost preparing for his exit from the I.L.P. I think he would welcome a really conclusive reason for joining the Liberal Party. Snowden is ill, some say very ill, at once bitter and apathetic; Keir Hardie 'used up', with no real faith left in the Labour Movement as a revolutionary force. Jowett — that dear, modest, dull but devotedly pious Socialist — shone out among his cleverer brethren and carried his unpractical resolution that Labour Members ought, on all questions and at all times, to vote 'according to the merits' of the particular issue before the House. The rank and file are puzzled and disheartened, and some of the delegates were seen to be weeping when Snowden fiercely attacked his colleagues of the Parliamentary Labour Party. The cold truth is that the Labour Members have utterly failed to impress the House of Commons and the constituencies as a live force, and have lost confidence in themselves and each other. The Labour Movement rolls on — the Trade Unions are swelling in membership and funds, more candidates are being put forward; but the faith of politically active members is becoming dim or confused whilst the rank and file become every day more restive. There is little leadership but a great deal of anti-leadership.

From *Beatrice Webb's Diaries* (**115**, p. 23).

Labour's war aims 1917

The general introductory statements below were followed by comments on the major territorial problems of a future peace settlement.

STATEMENT OF WAR AIMS OF THE LABOUR PARTY

As adopted at a joint conference of the societies affiliated with the British Trades Union Congress and the British Labour Party at Central Hall, Westminster, on December 28, 1917.

1. *The War*

The British Labour movement sees no reason to depart from the declaration unanimously agreed to at the Conference of the Socialist and Labour Parties of the Allied Nations on February 14, 1915, and it reaffirms that declaration. Whatever may have been the causes of the outbreak of war, it is clear that the peoples of Europe, who are necessarily the chief sufferers from its horrors, had themselves no hand in it. Their common interest is now so to conduct the terrible struggle in which they find themselves engaged as to bring it, as soon as may be possible, to an issue in a secure and lasting peace for the world.

2. *Making the world safe for democracy*

Whatever may have been the causes for which the war was begun, the fundamental purpose of the British Labour movement in supporting the continuance of the struggle is that the world may henceforth be made safe for democracy.

·   Of all the war aims, none is so important to the peoples of the world as that there shall be henceforth on earth no more war. Whoever triumphs, the people will have lost unless some effective method of preventing war can be found.

As means to this end, the British Labour movement relies very largely upon the complete democratisation of all countries; on the frank abandonment of every form of Imperialism; on the suppression of secret diplomacy, and on the placing of foreign policy, just as much as home policy, under the control of popularly elected Legislatures; on the absolute responsibility of the Foreign Minister of each country to its Legislature; on such concerted action as may be possible for the universal abolition of compulsory military service in all countries, the common limitation of the costly armaments by which all peoples are burdened, and the entire abolition of profit-making armament firms, whose pecuniary interest lies always in war scares and rivalry in preparation for war.

But it demands, in addition, that it should be an essential part of the treaty of peace itself that there should be forthwith established a Supernational Authority, or League of Nations, which should not only be adhered to by all the present belligerents, but which every other independent sovereign state in the world should be pressed to join; the immediate establishment of such League of Nations not only of an International High Court for the settlement of all disputes between states that are of justiciable nature, but also of appropriate machinery for prompt and effective mediation between states at issue that are not justiciable; the formation of an International Legislature, in which the representatives of every civilised state would have their allotted share; the gradual development, as far as may prove to be possible, of international legislation agreed to by and definitely binding upon the several states, and for a solemn agreement and pledge by all states that every issue between any two or more of them shall be submitted for settlement as aforesaid, and that they will all make common cause against any state which fails to adhere to this agreement.

3. *Territorial adjustments*

The British Labour movement has no sympathy with the attempts made, now in this quarter and now in that, to convert this war into a war of conquest, whether what is sought to be acquired by force is territory or wealth, nor should the struggle be prolonged for a single day, once the conditions of a permanent peace can be secured, merely for the sake of extending the boundaries of any state.

But it is impossible to ignore the fact that, not only restitution and reparation, but also certain territorial readjustments are required if a renewal of armaments and war is to be avoided. These readjustments must be such as can be arrived at by common agreement on the general principle of allowing all people to settle their own destinies, and for the purpose of removing any obvious cause of future international conflict.

(5, pp. 318-20.)

The 1918 Constitution

The following is the most important section of the new Labour Party Constitution of 1918 – mainly the work of Sidney Webb. The famous Clause Four (section 3d) at last committed the party to Socialism.

LABOUR PARTY CONSTITUTION OF 1918

1. *Name*
The Labour Party.

2. *Membership*
The Labour Party shall consist of all its affiliated organisations,* together with those men and women who are individual members of a Local Labour Party and who subscribe to the Constitution and Programme of the Party.

3. *Party Objects*
National

(*a*) To organise and maintain in Parliament and in the country a Political Labour Party, and to ensure the establishment of a Local Labour Party in every County Constituency and every Parliamentary Borough, with suitable divisional organisation in the separate constituencies of Divided Boroughs;

(*b*) To co-operate with the Parliamentary Committee of the Trades Union Congress, or other Kindred Organisations, in joint political or other action in harmony with the Party Constitution and Standing Orders;

(*c*) To give effect as far as may be practicable to the principles from time to time approved by the Party Conference;

(*d*) To secure for the producers by hand or by brain the full fruits of their industry, and the most equitable distribution thereof that may be possible, upon the basis of the common ownership of the means of production and the best obtainable system of popular administration and control of each industry or service;

* Trade Unions, Socialist Societies, Co-operative Societies, Trades Councils, and Local Labour Parties.

(*e*) Generally to promote the Political, Social, and Economic Emancipation of the People, and more particularly of those who depend directly upon their own exertions by hand or by brain for the means of life.

(5, pp. 326-27.)

document 20

From Liberalism to Labour

C. P. Trevelyan, son of the famous Victorian Liberal and brother of the historian, was before 1914 a radical Liberal M.P. He joined the Labour Party after the war, and subsequently served as Minister of Education in the first and second Labour Governments. This extract shows the key importance of foreign affairs (and therefore of the Union of Democratic Control) in driving a number of distinguished Liberals into the Labour Party.

Historians and philosophers, like catch-penny *Daily Mail* scrawlers, proclaimed the sole guilt of Germany, or raved at the brutalities in Belgium as proof of superhuman devilry in the Germans. But when offences against humanity were committed by the Allied Governments, they showed the same want of courage or the same narrowness of vision as the German professors whom they were always denouncing. What collective protest of Liberal intellectuals was there against the slaughter of the children at Karlsruhe, against the looting of Hungary, or against the supreme atrocity of the starvation of Central Europe? The one clear note which they tried to strike early in the war was the right of all peoples to self-determination. They called for sympathy for Croats and Czecho-Slovaks and Italians under Austrian rule. They demanded the independence of Poland. But when Europe began to be repartitioned at Paris, and a dozen new oppressions were substituted for the old ones, there was no protest in the name of principle or justice or Liberalism against the fate of Germans annexed to Poland, Austrians to Italy and Czecho-Slovakia, Serbs and Hungarians to Roumania, Bulgarians to Serbia, and the other patent outrages to national feeling created by the new settlement. Liberalism did not even insist on the application of the full principle of nationalism on which it had staked everything in the war. It marched behind the triumphal car of the reactionaries and accepted the old interpretation of nationalism, which is justice for the victors. No great leading light for a torn and distracted world shone from learned and cultivated Liberal England.

This, then, is the first great factor in the present situation, that as a bulwark against the tide of reaction and militarism which has swept the governing classes of the victorious nations along, the Liberals are useless. Their Liberal 'war to end war' has closed with an imperialist peace to perpetuate national injustice and armaments. And they have acquiesced.

From C. P. Trevelyan, *From Liberalism to Labour*, London 1921, pp. 56-8.

document 21
The Webbs on the First Labour Government

Sidney Webb was made President of the Board of Trade in the First Labour Government, and, as Lord Passfield, Colonial Secretary in the Second. He always had a great respect for MacDonald. Beatrice's attitude, however, was always more ambivalent: she despised MacDonald's mind and outlook, yet again and again reluctant admiration breaks in! See, for example, apart from the extract below, document 23.

[a] At the first meeting we found our respective places arranged at the historic long oblong table in the room at 10 Downing Street which John Bright had shown once to John Morley as the place where more villainy had been done than anywhere else in England — the P.M. in the middle of one long side, with the Lord Chancellor opposite to him; on his right Hankey and on his left the Chancellor of the Exchequer; all the rest being arranged apparently at haphazard. Haldane at once jumped in full of geniality with a lesson in manners; that we were always to address MacDonald as Mr. Prime Minister, but to refer to everyone else by his surname or title, without prefix. This was almost uniformly observed. The P.M. made hardly any preliminary observations, and plunged straight into business. Thomas began at once to smoke — or came in smoking, I forget which; and we silently made our first new precedent by allowing smoking, even pipes, from the very outset. Previous Cabinets during this

century had smoked only on rare occasions when they sat after 4 p.m. I imagine that, prior to 1900, smoking in Cabinet was undreamt of. What would Mr. G. have said? Except Trevelyan, nearly all the Labour Cabinet sometimes smoked; and many did so pretty continuously.

The Prime Minister's behaviour in Cabinet was perfect. He was never discourteous, never overbearing, never unduly dogmatic, patient to everyone, watchful to give everyone a chance to speak; and nevertheless quick to close the debate as soon as it was proper to do so, with his own summary of 'the sense of the meeting'. I think that the rest of us also behaved well. We certainly never quarrelled, never wrangled with each other, scarcely ever improperly interrupted each other or jeered at each other, even good-humouredly.

From Sidney Webb, 'The First Labour Government' (81).

[b] And it is clear that the P.M. is playing-up — without any kind of consultation with the majority of his colleagues or scruple or squeamishness about first pronouncements — towards the formation of a Centre Party — far less definitely Socialist in home affairs, far less distinctly pacifist in foreign affairs, say than Sidney would be if he were Prime Minister. MacDonald wants 8 million voters behind him and means to get them even if this entails shedding the I.L.P., the idealistically revolutionary section who pushed him into power. That ladder will be kicked down! MacDonald is in fact returning to his policy of 1910-14, as we always foresaw he would; but with a different facet. In those years he was willing to merge the Labour Party in the Liberal Party: to-day he realises that the Liberal Party is dead; so he is attracting, by his newly-won prestige and personal magnetism, the Conservative Collectivist element — but he insists that his collectivists shall dub themselves 'Labour' and accept him as their Leader. I do not accuse him of treachery: for he was never a Socialist, either revolutionary like Lansbury or administrative like the Webbs; he was always a believer in individualist political democracy tempered in its expression by Utopian Socialism. Where he has lacked integrity is in *posing* as a Socialist, and occasionally using revolutionary jargon. If he succeeds in getting a majority of the electors into this revised version of reformist conservatism embodied

117

in the Labour Party machine, things will move forward; the underlying assumptions will be changed by the rank and file workers, and the structure will necessarily adapt itself to the new outlook. It is another form of the famous policy of permeation, far more Machiavellian than that of the Webbs. But it will mean a new group rising up on the left to fight the Labour Party on the ground that it has denied the out-and-out Socialism the I.L.P. pretended to stand for. . . . But it hurts my pride to see the Fabian policy of permeation 'guyed' by MacDonald. Yet as a political performer he is showing himself a consummate artist. We had never realised that he had genius in this direction.

From *Beatrice Webb's Diaries* (**116**, p. 14).

document 22

The Zinoviev letter

This is an extract from the famous letter that is believed to have contributed to the Labour defeat in 1924. Zinoviev was President of the Comintern − the international organisation of world communist parties centred in Moscow − McManus, a British member. The latest opinion is that the letter was a forgery (see **58**).

Executive Committee,   Very Secret
   Third Communist International.
                             To the Central Committee,
                             British Communist Party.
Presidium,
   September 15th, 1924.
     Moscow.

Dear Comrades,
   The time is approaching for the Parliament of England to consider the Treaty concluded between the Governments of Great Britain and the S.S.S.R. for the purpose of ratification. . . .
   It is indispensable to stir up the masses of the British proletariat to bring into movement the army of unemployed proletarians whose position can be improved only after a loan has been granted to the S.S.S.R. . . . A settlement of relations

between the two countries will assist in the revolutionising of the international and British proletariat not less than a successful rising in any of the working districts of England, as the establishment of close contact between the British and Russian proletariat, the exchange of delegations and workers, etc., will make it possible for us to extend and develop the propaganda of ideas of Leninism in England and the Colonies. Armed warfare must be preceded by a struggle against the inclinations to compromise which are embedded among the majority of British workmen, against the ideas of evolution and peaceful extermination of capitalism. Only then will it be possible to count upon complete success of an armed insurrection. . . .

Form a directing operative head of the Military Section.

Do not put this off to a future moment, which may be pregnant with events and catch you unprepared.

Desiring you all success, both in organisation and in your struggle.

With Communist Greetings,
President of the Presidium of the I.K.K.I.
ZINOVIEV

Member of the Presidium: McMANUS.
Secretary: KUUSINEN.

(58, pp. xi-xiii.)

document 23

Beatrice Webb on Ramsay MacDonald 1926

The leader of the Labour Party was in his best form. He is an attractive creature; he has a certain beauty in colouring, figure and face, a delightful voice and an easy unpretentious manner, a youthful enjoyment of his prestige as a Prime Minister, all of which is amusing to watch. But his conversation is not entertaining or stimulating — it consists of pleasant anecdotes about political and society personages — occasionally some episode in his own career — told with calculated discretion. When he and I walked round the garden together he talked exclusively about his weekly visits to Christie's and the pieces of old furniture he was picking up. Directly you turn the conversation off trivial personalities on to subjects, whether it be general questions or the domestic problems of the Labour Party, J.R.M. dries up and looks bored. Not once did we *discuss* anything whatsoever and even the anecdotes led nowhere. Does he ever exchange ideas? Certainly not with us. At the gathering he looked cheery and he spoke well and at the farewell message his words were lit up by affectionate intimacy and homely wit which delighted his audience. My general impression is that J.R.M. feels himself to be *the* indispensable leader of a new political party which is bound to come into office within his life-time — a correct forecast, I think. He is no longer *intent* on social reform — any indignation he ever had at the present distribution of wealth he has lost; his real and intimate life is associating with non-political aristocratic society, surrounded with the beauty and dignity which wealth can buy and social experience can direct. Ramsay MacDonald is not distinguished either in intellect or character, and he has some very mean traits in his nature. But he has great gifts as a political leader, he has personal charm, he has vitality, he is assiduous, self-controlled and skilful.

From *Beatrice Webb's Diaries* (**116**, p. 111)

document 24

The end of the Second Labour Government

At noon on 24 August 1931 Ramsay MacDonald had informed the Labour Cabinet of his decision to head a National Government. That afternoon he arranged to see the other ministers: Hugh Dalton, a Junior Minister in the second Labour Government, describes the scene.

'At 2.30 the Cabinet Room is crowded. All Ministers not in the Cabinet, and all Whips, are invited. J.R.M. sits alone on the other side of the long table'. It is as though a martyr was speaking, just before a cruel death. 'He had originally summoned us, he says, to tell us that our salaries were to be cut. (This is not true, for the summonses went out only yesterday evening, when the "National" Government was already decided on.) But now he has to tell us that the Government is at an end. He is very sorry. We shall curse him, and he is afraid that he has caused us great embarrassment. But the gravity of the crisis is not yet widely understood. We shall be told that it is a bankers' ramp. But that is quite untrue. He has received most valuable help from the bankers. No one, for instance, could have been more helpful than the two representatives of the Bank of England. "Poor Norman has broken down under the strain." It was quite essential to get a loan quickly. Otherwise sterling would have collapsed. There would have been a run on the banks, and then a run on the Post Office. . . .

'He thinks the crisis could have been avoided if the Cabinet hadn't changed its mind at a critical point. A plan had been drawn up and agreed, which would have sufficed to secure the loan required. But then the Cabinet went back on it. (This also is untrue and is much resented by Uncle and others, when it is reported to them.) This made necessary a Government of Persons, not of Parties. He is going through with this. He has not called us here in order to try to form any cave, or to ask us to join him. Most of us are young men, with our political careers before us. He realises that he is committing political suicide. He is not going to ask any of us to do the same, or to put our heads into the noose into which he will put his. But . . . perhaps some of us *would* be willing to travel the same road with him. . . .

'Then a question or two. Attlee asks what would be done to the rentiers. He can't answer that. It is impossible to anticipate a Budget statement. Shinwell asks whether the alternative was considered of the Cabinet resigning and leaving to the Tories and Liberals the responsibility of carrying through an economy policy. Oh, yes. Every possible alternative has been considered. Susan Lawrence asks whether formal resignations by Junior Ministers are necessary. Oh, no. All members of the Government will resign together, and then the new administration will be formed.

'And then we disperse. Going out, Willy Lunn and I speak vigorously against J.R.M. And I apparently am clearly audible, for a colleague claws my sleeve nervously and says: "Don't speak so loud. There are a lot of Pressmen outside. They will hear you." And I reply: "I don't give a damn if they do!" To one Pressman I say: "Just for a handful of panic he left us!" and to another: "I am going into opposition now." And so, by all the signs, are the great majority of us'.

From Hugh Dalton, *Call Back Yesterday* (**118**, pp. 272-3).

Labour and foreign policy

The major debate of the 1935 Labour Party Conference was on the Executive's resolution in favour of economic sanctions against Italy, over her invasion of Abyssinia. Cripps and Lansbury opposed: Ernest Bevin denounced the latter's pacifist speech in the famous words quoted below.

I think the Movement ought to understand the Trade Union Congress's position. Let me remind the delegates that, when George Lansbury says what he has said today in the Conference, it is rather late to say it, and I hope this Conference will not be influenced by either sentiment or personal attachment. I hope you will carry no resolution of an emergency character telling a man with a conscience like Lansbury what he ought to do. . . . It is placing the Executive and the Movement in an absolutely wrong position to be taking your conscience round from body to body asking to be told what you ought to do with it . . . I have had to sit in Conference with the Leader and come to decisions, and I am a democrat and I feel we have been betrayed.

From the *Report of the 1935 Labour Party Conference.*

The Labour Party electoral manifesto 1945

The following is part of the industrial section of the Labour Manifesto, Let Us Face the Future, *for which Herbert Morrison was mainly responsible.*

What will the Labour Party do?

First, the whole of the national resources, in land, material and labour must be fully employed. Production must be raised to the highest level and related to purchasing power. Over-production is not the cause of depression and unemployment; it is under-consumption that is responsible. It is doubtful whether we have ever, except in war, used the whole of our productive capacity. This must be corrected because, upon our ability to produce and organise a fair and generous distribution of the product, the standard of living of our people depends.

Secondly, a high and constant purchasing power can be maintained through good wages, social services and insurance, and taxation which bears less heavily on the lower-income groups. But everybody knows that money and savings lose their value if prices rise, so rents and the prices of the necessities of life will be controlled.

Thirdly, planned investment in essential industries and on houses, schools, hospitals and civic centres will occupy a large field of capital expenditure. A National Investment Board will determine social priorities and promote better timing in private investment. In suitable cases we would transfer the use of efficient Government factories from war production to meet the needs of peace. The location of new factories will be suitably controlled, and where necessary the Government will itself build factories. There must be no depressed areas in the New Britain.

Fourthly, the Bank of England with its financial powers must be brought under public ownership, and the operations of the other banks harmonised with industrial needs.

By these and other means full employment can be achieved. But a policy of Jobs for All must be associated with a policy of general economic expansion and efficiency as set out in the next section of this Declaration. Indeed, it is not enough to ensure that there are jobs for all. If the standard of life is to be high — as it should be — the standard of production must be high. This means that industry must be thoroughly efficient if the needs of the nation are to be met.

The Labour Party is a Socialist Party, and proud of it. Its ultimate purpose at home is the establishment of the Socialist Commonwealth of Great Britain — free, democratic, efficient, progressive, public-spirited, its material resources organised in the service of the British people.

But Socialism cannot come overnight, as the product of a week-end revolution. The members of the Labour Party, like the British people, are practical-minded men and women.

There are basic industries ripe and over-ripe for public ownership and management in the direct service of the nation. There are many smaller businesses rendering good service which can be left to go on with their useful work.

There are big industries not yet ripe for public ownership

which must nevertheless be required by constructive super-vision to further the nation's needs and not to prejudice national interests by restrictive anti-social monopoly or cartel agreements — caring for their own capital structures and profits at the cost of a lower standard of living for all.

In the light of these considerations, the Labour Party submits to the nation the following industrial programme:

1. Public ownership of the fuel and power industries. For a quarter of a century the coal industry, producing Britain's most precious national raw material, has been floundering chaotically under the ownership of many hundreds of inde-pendent companies. Amalgamation under public ownership will bring great economies in operation and make it possible to modernise production methods and to raise safety stan-dards in every colliery in the country. Public ownership of gas and electricity undertakings will lower charges, prevent competitive waste, open the way for co-ordinated research and development, and lead to the reforming of uneconomic areas of distribution. Other industries will benefit.

2. Public ownership of inland transport. Co-ordination of transport services by rail, road, air and canal cannot be achieved without unification. And unification without public ownership means a steady struggle with sectional interests or the enthronement of a private monopoly, which would be a menace to the rest of industry.

3. Public ownership of iron and steel. Private monopoly has maintained high prices and kept inefficient high-cost plants in' existence. Only if public ownership replaces private mon-opoly can the industry become efficient.

These socialised industries, taken over on a basis of fair compensation, to be conducted efficiently in the interests of consumers, coupled with proper status and conditions for the workers employed in them.

4. Public supervision of monopolies and cartels with the aim of advancing industrial efficiency in the service of the nation. Anti-social restrictive practices will be prohibited.

5. A firm and clear-cut programme for the export trade.

From *Let us Face the Future: A Declaration of Labour Policy for the Consideration of the Nation*, 1945.

Labour in power 1945

The following is the concluding section of Hugh Dalton's second volume of memoirs. He was appointed Chancellor of the Exchequer in the 1945 Labour Government.

In the first division of the Parliament, on August 17th, on a motion to take Private Members' time for the sake of the Government's programme, we won by 329 to 142. A glorious new sensation! And the names of the Government supporters in the Aye Lobby read, to me, like a triumphant reverberating roll-call.

Till now, since the election, there had been only skirmishing. But now the battle was joined.

So we went, each of us to his battle station, and I to the Treasury, to encounter most grave problems, wide opportunities, heavy strains, hard choices. But through it all I was to be sustained by the strength and comradeship and understanding of our great Parliamentary majority. And we all knew that, within us, and because of us, and around us, something had suddenly changed.

> *England arise, the long, long night is over;*
> *Faint in the East behold the dawn appear.*

Edward Carpenter's Socialist Hymn at last had found fulfilment. After the long storm of war, after the short storm of election, we saw the sunrise. As we had sung in the shadows, so now in the light,

> *England is risen and the day is here.*

From Hugh Dalton, *The Fateful Years* (**119**, pp. 482-3).

Appendix: The Labour Vote

Elections	Votes	M.P.s elected	Candidates	% share of total vote
1900	63,304	2	15	1·8
1906	329,748	30	51	5·9
1910 (Jan.)	505,657	40	78	7·6
1910 (Dec.)	371,772	42	56	7·1
1918	2,385,472	63	388	22·2
1922	4,241,383	142	411	29·5
1923	4,438,508	191	422	30·5
1924	5,489,077	151	512	33·0
1929	8,389,512	288	571	37·1
1931	6,649,630	52	515	30·6
1935	8,325,491	154	552	37·9
1945	11,995,152	393	604	47·8

Bibliography

DOCUMENTS

1 Bealey, Frank, ed. *The Social and Political Thought of the British Labour Party*, Weidenfeld & Nicolson, 1970.

2 Beattie, Alan, ed. *English Party Politics*, 2 vols, Weidenfeld & Nicolson, 1970.

3 Craig, F. W. S., ed. *British General Election Manifestoes 1918-1966*, Political Reference Publications, Chichester, 1970.

4 Hobsbawm, Eric, ed. *Labour's Turning Point 1880-1900*, Lawrence & Wishart, 1948.

5 Stansky, Peter, ed. *The Left and War: The British Labour Party and World War I*, Oxford University Press, 1969.

POLITICAL AND ECONOMIC DEVELOPMENT

6 Adelman, Paul. *Gladstone, Disraeli and Later Victorian Politics*, Seminar Studies in History, Longman, 1970.

7 Beer, Samuel H. *Modern British Politics*, Faber, 1965.

8 Butler, David and Freeman, Jennie. *British Political Facts 1900-1968*, Macmillan, 2nd rev. edn, 1969: an indispensable reference book.

9 Checkland, S. G. *The Rise of Industrial Society in England 1815-1885*, Longman, 1964.

10 Clarke, P. F. *Lancashire and the New Liberalism*, Cambridge University Press, 1971.

11 Cook, Chris. 'A Stranger Death of Liberal England', in *Lloyd George. Twelve essays*, ed. A. J. P. Taylor, Hamish Hamilton, 1971.

12 Dangerfield, George. *The Strange Death of Liberal England* (Constable, 1935), Paladin Books edn, 1970.

13 Halévy, Elie. *A History of the English People in the Nineteenth Century*, vol. 5, *1895-1905*, and vol. 6, *1905-1914*, Benn, 1926.

14 Halévy, Elie. *The Era of Tyrannies*, Allen Lane, The Penguin Press, 1967: contains a number of penetrating essays on the British Labour Movement.

127

15 Hobsbawm, Eric. *Industry and Empire. An Economic History of Britain since 1750*, Weidenfeld & Nicolson, 1968; Penguin Books edn, 1969: especially stimulating for Labour history.

16 Jenkins, Roy. *Mr Balfour's Poodle*, Heinemann, 1954.

17 Lynd, Helen Merrell. *England in the Eighteen-Eighties* (Oxford University Press, 1945), Cass, reprint edn, 1968: useful on ideas.

18 Marx, Karl and Engels, F. *On Britain*, Moscow 1953.

19 Marwick, Arthur. *The Deluge. British Society and the First World War* (Bodley Head, 1965), Penguin Books edn, 1967: a pioneer attempt at the social history of war.

20 McCallum, R. B. and Readman, Alison. *The British General Election of 1945*, Oxford University Press, 1947.

21 McKenzie, Robert. *British Political Parties*, Heinemann, 2nd edn, 1964.

22 Medlicott, W. N. *Contemporary England 1914-64*, Longman, 1967.

23 Mowat, C. L. *Britain between the Wars 1918-1940*, Methuen, 1955.

24 Orwell, George. *The Road to Wigan Pier*, Gollancz, 1937: a classic study of working-class life during the Depression.

25 Pelling, Henry. *The Social Geography of British Elections 1885-1910*, Macmillan, 1967.

26 Pelling, Henry. *Popular Politics and Society in Late Victorian Britain*, Macmillan, 1968.

27 Pelling, Henry. *Britain and the Second World War*, Collins, Fontana, 1970.

28 Perkin, Harold. *The Origins of Modern English Society 1780-1880*, Routledge, 1969.

29 Swartz, Marvin. *The Union of Democratic Control during the First World War*, Oxford University Press, 1971.

30 Taylor, A. J. P. *English History 1914-1945*, Oxford University Press, 1965.

31 Wilson, Trevor. *The Downfall of the Liberal Party 1918-35* (Collins, 1966), Fontana edn, 1968: an outstanding contribution to the story of Liberal decline.

SOCIALISM

32 Beer, Max. *A History of British Socialism*, Allen & Unwin, 1940.

33 Blatchford, Robert. *Merrie England*, London, 1895: a socialist classic.

34 Clayton, Joseph. *The Rise and Decline of Socialism in Great Britain 1884-1924*, Faber, 1926.

35 Cole, Margaret. *The Story of Fabian Socialism*, Heinemann, 1961: exaggerates Fabian influence.

36 Ensor, R. C. K. 'Permeation', in *The Webbs and their Work*, ed. Margaret Cole, Muller, 1949.

37 *Fabian Essays* (1889), Jubilee edn, Allen & Unwin, 1948: a landmark in British socialist thought.

38 Fremantle, Anne. *This Little Band of Prophets. The Story of the Gentle Fabians*, Allen & Unwin, 1960.

39 Gray, Alexander. *The Socialist Tradition*, Longman, 1947: witty and iconoclastic.

40 Hobson, J. A. 'The influence of Henry George in England', *Fortnightly Review*, vol. 62, 1897.

41 Hyndman, H. M. *England for All*, E. W. Allen, 1881: Marxism *à la* Hyndman.

42 Jones, Peter d'A. *The Christian Socialist Revival*, Princeton University Press, 1968.

43 Lee, H. W. and Archbold, E. *Social-Democracy in Britain*, London, 1935: pro-S.D.F.

44 MacDonald, J. R. *The Socialist Movement*, Butterworth, 1911.

45 McBriar, A. M. *Fabian Socialism and English Politics 1884-1918*, Cambridge University Press, 1962: a scholarly debunking.

46 Pease, Edward R. *The History of the Fabian Society* (1916), Cass reprint, 1963: the standard history of its greatest days.

47 Pelling, Henry. *America and the British Left*, Black, 1956.

48 Shaw, G. B. 'Early days', in *The Webbs and their Work*, ed. Margaret Cole, Muller, 1949.

49 Shaw, G. B. *Essays in Fabian Socialism*, Constable, 1932.

50 Thompson, Laurence. *The Enthusiasts*, Gollancz, 1971: the lives of the late-Victorian socialists, Katherine and John Glasier.

THE LABOUR PARTY

51 Adams, W. S. 'Lloyd George and the Labour Party', *Past and Present*, vol. 1, 1952-3.

52 Bassett, Reginald. *Nineteen Thirty-One. Political crisis*, Macmillan, 1958: a meticulous study, strongly pro-MacDonald.

53 Bealey, Frank. 'Negotiations between the Liberal Party and the Labour Representation Committee before the general election of 1906', *Bulletin of the Institute of Historical Research*, vol. 29/30, 1956/7.

54 Bealey, Frank and Pelling, Henry. *Labour and Politics, 1900-1906*, Oxford University Press, 1958: a study of the L.R.C.

55 Brand, Carl F. *British Labour's Rise to Power*, Stanford University Press, 1941: specialist essays.

56 Brand, Carl F. *The British Labour Party. A Short History*, Stanford University Press, 1965: a clear narrative.

57 Carlton, David. *MacDonald versus Henderson. The Foreign Policy of the Second Labour Government*, Macmillan, 1970.

58 Chester, Lewis, Fay, Stephen and Young, Hugo. *The Zinoviev Letter*, Heinemann, 1967.

59 Cline, C. A. *Recruits to Labour. The British Labour Party 1914-31*, Syracuse University Press, 1963: the Liberal emigration into the Labour Party.

60 Cole, G. D. H. *A History of the Labour Party since 1914*, Allen & Unwin, 1948: the standard work.

61 Cowling, Maurice. *The Impact of Labour 1920-1924*, Cambridge University Press, 1971: narrowly political.

62 Cripps, Stafford. *The Struggle for Peace*, Gollancz, 1936: a compendium of left-wing delusions.

63 Duffy, A. E. P. 'Differing policies and personal rivalries in the origins of the Independent Labour Party', *Victorian Studies*, vol. 6, 1962/3.

64 Elton, Godfrey. *'England, Arise!'*, Cape, 1931: a vividly written account of the late-Victorian Labour Movement.

65 Graubard, S. R. *British Labour and the Russian Revolution 1917-24*, Harvard University Press, 1956.

66 Howard, Anthony. 'We are the masters now', in *Age of Austerity*, ed. Michael Sissons and Philip French, Hodder & Stoughton, 1963: the 1945 general election.

67 Lyman, R. W. *The First Labour Government 1924*, Chapman & Hall, 1957.

68 Lyman, R. W. 'James Ramsay MacDonald and the leadership of the Labour Party 1918-1922', *Journal of British Studies*, vol. 2, 1962/3.

69 Lyman, R. W. 'The British Labour Party: the conflict between Socialist ideals and practical politics between the wars', *Journal of British Studies*, vol. 5, 1965/6.

70 McHenry, Dean E. *The Labour Party in Transition 1931-1938*, Routledge, 1938.

71 McKibbin, R. I. 'James Ramsay MacDonald and the problem of the independence of the Labour Party 1910-1914', *Journal of Modern History*, vol. 42, 1970.

72 Miliband, Ralph. *Parliamentary Socialism. A study in the politics of Labour*, Allen & Unwin, 1961: a left-wing view.

73 Naylor, John F. *Labour's International Policy. The Labour Party in the 1930's*, Weidenfeld & Nicolson, 1969: a first-class study of Labour's quarrels over foreign affairs.

74 Pelling, Henry. *A Short History of the Labour Party*, Macmillan, 3rd edn, 1968.

75 Pelling, Henry. *The Origins of the Labour Party 1880-1900*, Oxford University Press, 2nd edn, 1965: the standard work.

76 Poirier, Philip P. *The Advent of the Labour Party*, Allen & Unwin, 1958: an excellent American study; goes up to 1906.

77 Skidelsky, Robert. *Politicians and the Slump. The Labour Government of 1929-1931* (Macmillan, 1967), Penguin Books edn, 1970: *the* outstanding recent study.

78 Skidelsky, Robert. 'Crisis 1931', *The Times*, 3/4 December 1968: adds some details to (77) from the Cabinet Papers.

79 Skidelsky, Robert. '1929-1931 revisited', *Society for the Study of Labour History Bulletin*, no. 21, Autumn 1970: modifies the thesis over Labour failure contained in (77).

80 Thompson, Paul. *Socialists, Liberals and Labour. The struggle for London 1885-1914*, Routledge, 1967: one of the few regional studies.

81 Webb, Sidney. 'The First Labour Government', *The Political Quarterly*, vol. 32, 1961: by a distinguished member.

82 Winkler, Henry R. 'The emergence of a Labour foreign policy in Great Britain, 1918-29', *Journal of Modern History*, vol. 28, 1956.

THE LABOUR MOVEMENT

83 Allen, V. L. 'The reorganisation of the Trade Union Congress, 1918-1927', *The British Journal of Sociology*, vol. 11, 1960.

84 Clegg, H. A., Fox, Alan and Thompson, A. F. *A History of British Trades Unions since 1889, Volume I, 1889-1910*, Oxford University Press, 1964: the most important history since the Webbs'.

85 Cole, G. D. H. *A Short History of the British Working-Class Movement 1789-1947*, Allen & Unwin, 1948.

86 Cole, G. D. H. 'British Trade Unions in the third quarter of the nineteenth century', *International Review of Social History*, 1937.

87 Cole, G. D. H. *British Working Class Politics 1832-1914*, Routledge, 1941.

88 Dowse, Robert E. *Left in the Centre. The Independent Labour Party 1893-1940*, Longman, 1966: disappointing.

89 Duffy, A. E. P. 'New unionism in Britain, 1889-1890: a re-appraisal', *Economic History Review*, vol. 14, 1961/2.

90 Gregory, Roy. *The Miners and British Politics 1906-14*, Oxford University Press, 1968: important for Liberal/Labour relations.

91 Harrison, Martin. *Trade Unions and the Labour Party since 1945*, Allen & Unwin, 1960.

92 Hobsbawm, Eric. *Labouring Men*, Weidenfeld & Nicolson, 1968: contains major essays on New Unionism particularly.

93 Howell, George. *Trade Unionism New and Old*, Methuen, 1891.

94 Hutt, Allen. *The Post-War History of the British Working Class*, Gollancz, 1937: Communist.

95 Kendall, Walter. *The Revolutionary Movement in Britain 1900-21*, Weidenfeld & Nicolson, 1969: the 'lost causes' of British labour history.

96 Lewis, John. *The Left Book Club*, Gollancz, 1970.

97 Lovell, John. *Stevedores and Dockers. A study of trade unionism in the Port of London, 1870-1914*, Macmillan, 1969.

98 Macfarlane, L. J. *The British Communist Party. Its origins and development until 1929*, MacGibbon and Kee, 1966.

99 Mann, Tom and Tillett, Ben. *The 'New' Trades Unionism*, London, 1890.

100 Marwick, Arthur. 'The Independent Labour Party in the nineteen-twenties', *Bulletin of the Institute of Historical Research*, vol. 35, 1962.

101 Middlemas, Robert K. *The Clydesiders*, Hutchinson, 1965.

102 Pelling, Henry. *A History of British Trade Unionism*, Penguin Books, 1963: the best short history.

103 Pelling, Henry. *The British Communist Party. A historical profile*, Black, 1958.

104 Phelps Brown, E. H. *The Growth of British Industrial Relations. A study from the standpoint of 1906-14*, Macmillan, 1959.

105 Pribicevic, B. *The Shop Stewards' Movement and Workers' Control 1910-1922*, Blackwell, 1959.

106 Roberts, B. C. *The Trades Union Congress 1868-1921*, Allen & Unwin, 1958.

107 Saville, John. 'Trade unions and free labour. The background to the Taff Vale decision', in *Essays in Labour History*, ed. Asa Briggs and John Saville, Macmillan, 1967.

108 Smith, H. Llewellyn and Nash, Vaughan. *The Story of the Dockers' Strike*, Fisher Unwin, 1889: the classic account.

109 Stafford, Ann. *A Match to Fire the Thames*, Hodder & Stoughton, 1961: a popular account of the labour struggles in the East End, 1887-89.

110 Symons, Julian. *The General Strike*, Cresset Press, 1957: a good popular account with much eye-witness material.

111 Webb, Sidney and Beatrice. *The History of Trade Unionism*, Longman, 1920 edn.

BIOGRAPHIES AND MEMOIRS

112 Barker, C. A. *Henry George*, New York, Oxford University Press, 1955.

113 Bullock, Alan. *The Life and Times of Ernest Bevin*, vols 1 and 2, Heinemann, 1960-67: probably the best biography of a British labour leader.

114 Clynes, J. R. *Memoirs*, 2 vols, Hutchinson, 1937.

115 Cole, Margaret, ed. *Beatrice Webb's Diaries, 1912-1924*, Longman, 1952.

116 Cole, Margaret, ed. *Beatrice Webb's Diaries, 1924-1932*, Longman, 1956.

117 Collison, William. *The Apostle of Free Labour. The Life Story of William Collison*, Hurst & Blackett, 1913.

118 Dalton, Hugh. *Call Back Yesterday, Memoirs 1887-1931*, Muller, 1953.

119 Dalton, Hugh. *The Fateful Years, Memoirs 1931-1945*, Muller, 1957: these two volumes provide one of the few entertaining and informative Labour autobiographies.

120 Elton (Godfrey), Lord. *The Life of James Ramsay MacDonald, 1866-1919*, Collins, 1939.

121 Foot, Michael. *Aneurin Bevan, vol. 1. 1887-1945*, MacGibbon & Kee, 1962.

122 Hamilton, Mary Agnes. *Arthur Henderson*, Heinemann, 1938.

123 Henderson, Philip, ed. *Letters of William Morris*, Longman, 1950.

124 Kent, W. *John Burns. Labour's lost leader*, Williams & Norgate, 1950.

125 Laurence, Dan H., ed. *Bernard Shaw. Collected Letters 1874-1897*, Max Reinhardt, 1965.

126 Mann, Tom. *Memoirs*, MacGibbon & Kee edn, 1967.

127 Morgan, K. O. *Keir Hardie*, Oxford University Press (Clarendon Biography), 1967: an excellent brief study.

128 Morrison (Herbert) Lord. *An Autobiography*, Odhams, 1960.

129 Mosley, Sir Oswald. *My Life*, Nelson, 1968.

130 Nicolson, Sir Harold. *King George V* (Constable, 1952), Pan Books edn, 1967: important for the first two Labour Governments.

131 Pelling, Henry. 'H. H. Champion: pioneer of labour representation', *The Cambridge Journal*, vol. 6, January 1953.

132 Snowden (Philip), Viscount. *An Autobiography*, 2 vols, Nicholson & Watson, 1934.

133 Stewart, William. *J. Keir Hardie*, London, 1925.

134 Thompson, Laurence. *Robert Blatchford: Portrait of an Englishman*, Gollancz, 1951.

135 Thorne, Will. *My Life's Battles*, G. Newnes, n.d.

136 Tillett, Ben. *Memories and Reflections*, John Long, 1931.

137 Torr, Dona. *Tom Mann and his Times*, vol. 1, 1856-1890, Laurence & Wishart, 1956.

138 Tsuzuki, C. *H. M. Hyndman and British Socialism*, Oxford University Press, 1961.

139 Webb, Beatrice. *My Apprenticeship*, 2 vols (Longman, 1950), Penguin Books edn, 1938: a great late-Victorian testament.

140 Webb, Beatrice. *Our Partnership*, ed. Barbara Drake and Margaret Cole, Longman, 1948.

141 Williams, Francis. *A Prime Minister Remembers. The War and Post-War Memoirs of Earl Attlee*, Heinemann, 1961.

Index